FRIENDS IN REAL LIFE

Finding Real Community in a Virtual World

Ryan Frank

Friends in Real Life: Finding Real Community in a Virtual World

© 2022 by Ryan Frank. All rights reserved.

Published by KidzMatter
432 East Val Lane, Marion, IN 46952

Printed in the United States of America

All rights reserved. No part of this publication may be reproduced, stored in a retrieval system, or transmitted in any form or by any means-for example, electronic, photocopy, recording-without the prior written permission of the publisher. The only exception is brief quotations in printed reviews.

Unless otherwise indicated, all Scripture quotations are from The ESV® Bible (The Holy Bible, English Standard Version®), copyright © 2001 by Crossway, a publishing ministry of Good News Publishers. Used by permission. All rights reserved.

Scripture quotations marked (NLT) are taken from the Holy Bible, New Living Translation, copyright © 1996, 2004, 2015 by Tyndale House Foundation. Used by permission of Tyndale House Publishers, Carol Stream, Illinois 60188, USA. All rights reserved.

Scripture quotations marked (MSG) are taken from the THE MESSAGE. Copyright © 1993, 1994, 1995, 1996, 2000, 2001, 2002. Used by permission of NavPress Publishing Group.

Scripture quotations marked (NIV) are taken from the Holy Bible, New International Version®, NIV®. Copyright © 1973, 1978, 1984, 2011 by Biblica, Inc.™ Used by permission of Zondervan. All rights reserved worldwide. www.zondervan.com The "NIV" and "New International Version" are trademarks registered in the United States Patent and Trademark Office by Biblica, Inc.™

Scripture quotations marked (NASB) are taken from the New American Standard Bible®, Copyright © 1960, 1971, 1977, 1995, 2020 by The Lockman Foundation. Used by permission. All rights reserved. www.lockman.org

Scripture quotations marked (KJV) are taken from The Authorized (King James) Version. Rights in the Authorized Version in the United Kingdom are vested in the Crown. Reproduced by permission of the Crown's patentee, Cambridge University Press.

Scripture quotations marked (TPT) are from The Passion Translation®. Copyright © 2017, 2018, 2020 by Passion & Fire Ministries, Inc. Used by permission. All rights reserved. ThePassionTranslation.com.

Scripture quotations marked (NCV) are taken from the New Century Version®. Copyright © 2005 by Thomas Nelson. Used by permission. All rights reserved.

Scripture quotations marked (CEB) are taken from the COMMON ENGLISH BIBLE. © Copyright 2011 COMMON ENGLISH BIBLE. All rights reserved. Used by permission. (www.CommonEnglishBible.com).

Scripture quotations marked (NRSV) are from the New Revised Standard Version Bible, copyright © 1989 National Council of the Churches of Christ in the United States of America. Used by permission. All rights reserved worldwide.

Scripture quotations marked (LEB) are from the Lexham English Bible. Copyright 2012 Logos Bible Software. Lexham is a registered trademark of Logos Bible Software.

979-8-9850095-0-7 (Hardback)
978-1-0879-8146-8 (ePub)

Cover design and interior layout by Nicole Jones - kneecoalgrace@gmail.com
Edited by Theda Crawford

▶DEDICATION

This book is dedicated to the children's ministry community. Beth and I are privileged to lead this amazing group of people and are thankful that God has chosen us.

▶TABLE OF CONTENTS

Foreword 9

Introduction 13

Do You Know Jack? 17

Proactively Joining God at Work 39

It Must Be More than Sunday 61

The Power of Teamwork 89

So Glad You're Here 115

Simply Encourage 139

Praising Through the Pain 161

It's a Team Sport 183

Don't Waste Your Loneliness 205

The Power of Mentorship 233

Conclusion 253

Endnotes 259

▶FOREWORD
BY BETH FRANK

As I sat down at my computer to write this foreword, I had lots of thoughts swirling. Thoughts about community... thoughts about Ryan... and thoughts on how the topic of community is so needed right now. I wasn't quite sure what direction to go, though. I believe that this message is one of utmost importance for the time in which we live. I also know that Ryan has lots to say on this topic. He has learned much from years of leading a growing online community and connecting people virtually as well physically. Then I decided that I should start where the book started. Back to when an idea blossomed from our own search for Friends in Real Life.

Let me take you back to the beginning of this project. It was one of those days that you will never forget. You will never forget because it was so good. Not good from a crazy, once-in-a-lifetime itinerary. It was good from the sweet simplicity of the day. Ryan and I had decided to carve out some much needed time away and snuck off to Florida in the spring. We were tired and desperately in need of some alone time.

Ryan and I do what we call adventure days. These are times where we just disappear off the grid for a day. Sometimes it really is an adventure and we will go hiking or exploring a "new to us" area. On this spring day in May, our adventure day was really just a day of quiet time together. We loaded up our Jeep with everything needed for a day at the beach and headed out. The weather was amazing and we found the perfect little spot of deserted beach. We just sat and talked and dreamed and planned and even napped. It was perfect in every way! That day we talked about some hard things in our own personal life. We were craving more community in areas of our life that were difficult. We also talked about ministry plans for the future. Ryan said he wanted to write a book to release the coming fall. He talked about a few ideas that were percolating in his head. But as the day wore on and our conversations kept returning to community and connections, a light bulb went off in my mind. I knew that God had been leading our conversations that day and that Ryan would do an amazing job writing about Biblical community in the context of a virtual world.

Isn't it just like God to lead you through a season because He is going to use what you have learned to share with others? Throughout Ryan's writing of this book, we have experienced some very alone times where we wondered where everyone was at. We have also experienced some mountaintop times of the best community in our entire lives. God has a plan and I know that He specifically had this journey for us to walk through so we could learn, grow, and share it with others.

I love the words in Exodus that say…

> "The Lord said, 'I have indeed seen the misery of my people in Egypt. I have heard them crying out because of their slave drivers, and I am concerned about their suffering. So I have come down to rescue them from the hand of the Egyptians and to bring them up out of that land into a good and spacious land, a land flowing with milk and honey.'"[1]

I love these verses because of what we learn about God here. It says He saw their misery, He heard their crying, and He was concerned. This caused God to act. Do you know the incredible thing about God's action? It was through Moses. God's plan to help His people was through another "people".

Community is God's plan for His people – including you. You and I were not made to do this life alone. God wants us to live life helping others and being helped. This is the real and raw stuff of life. Some of our greatest joys and deepest sorrows will come from living in community. People will most certainly disappoint and fail us, but this doesn't mean we should quit. No, it means we keep hold of our Savior's hand and decide to grab again the hand of our neighbor as we walk the journey of this life together. Because honestly, what a friend we have in Jesus and it's Him alone that makes these connections possible.

BTW... Hello, I'm Beth and I am definitely friends in real life with the author. We have been married for 23 adventure-filled years this year. I love doing life and community with him. Friend, I think you will love this book and what Ryan has to say about being Friends in Real Life.

XO,
Beth

▶INTRODUCTION

As a kid, I loved watching Gilligan's Island. I would race home from school to watch those seven castaways as they tried to survive being shipwrecked on an island. My favorite parts were watching Gilligan almost always unintentionally sabotage their attempts to escape the island.

I'll never forget the episode where a NASA satellite with a TV camera accidentally landed on the island instead of on Mars. They tried to communicate their S.O.S. when the camera was operational. However, thanks to a Gilligan goof-up, they were covered with glue and feathers, and the NASA scientists mistakenly believed they were seeing the first proof of life on Mars.

Gilligan's Island serves as a reminder that people were created with a deep need for belonging. Whether you are wealthy like the Howell's, sweet and innocent like MaryAnn, or a Movie-star like Ginger; no one wants to go through life alone.

From birth, we are wired to need other people. Newborns need a nurturing touch, reassuring voices, and gentle love to grow and thrive. As kids get older, they still need that trusted voice and affirming love. Into adulthood, we each long for relationships with people. This is all by God's design.

In the book of Genesis, we read about God creating Adam. Adam was living in a sinless paradise. He walked with God each day and enjoyed His fellowship. Even in a perfect world though, something was wrong. God said, "It is not good that the man should be alone; I will make him a helper fit for him."[1]

If Adam was in the presence of God every day – living in a perfect world – and was still alone, how much more do we need each other today?

At the beginning of time, God said it was not good for us to be alone. So He gave us relationships. He created you with a need for community. There is no way around it. He has a plan and purpose for you – and it includes others.

> There is no way around it. He has a plan and purpose for you - and it includes others.

We see community throughout the pages of the Bible. God Himself exists in community. Before the angels, before the universe, before time itself as we know it; the Father, Son, and Holy Spirit existed in community. God chose the Israelites to be His special people. They lived and worshiped Him in community. Following the death, resurrection, and ascension of Jesus; God instituted the church – a community of believers.

You don't have to live on an uncharted South Pacific island like Gilligan to sense a need for community. You can belong to a big family, go to church, be the most popular person in town, or have hundreds of friends on Facebook… and still be lonely.

We are more connected today than ever thanks to our phones and social media, yet we are lonelier than ever. This virtual world of ours improves our productivity, makes organizations run efficiently, and creates incredible opportunities for business and ministry. However, it has also created a lot of relationally-challenged people.

In this book, I want you to be reminded that God created you to do life with people. You need others to grow and develop your potential. The Bible says, "Whoever walks with the wise becomes wise, but the companion of fools suffers harm."[2] It also says, "As iron sharpens iron, so one man sharpens another."[3]

Several years ago, I heard Craig Groeschel say, "Show me your friends and I'll show you your future." Doing life with the right people is essential if you want to reach your full potential.

Rick Warren says:

> "There are some things you will never learn on your own. You only learn them in community. To grow and develop your potential, you must learn from other people.
>
> For instance, you can only learn forgiveness in relationships. You can't learn that on your own. You can only learn loyalty in relationships. You can only learn love in relationships. You can't learn kindness or faithfulness or graciousness or unselfishness without others.
>
> In fact, the most important things you need to learn in life require that you be in relationships with other people. You can't do it on your own. If you want to build your potential, you must learn from others."[4]

Throughout the ten chapters of this book, we will explore what it means to have friends in real life. In our culture, acquiring a friend is often reduced to a click or a touch on a screen. How do you build an authentic community in this virtual world? How do you move beyond surface-level relationships to real-life friends? The pathway is simple, but it's not always easy. Thankfully we have some guidance in the Bible.

> ▶ In our culture, acquiring a friend is often reduced to a click or a touch on a screen.

Over the 10 chapters of this book, we will examine the ministry of the Apostle Paul and the early church to see what community looked like back then and what we can learn some 2,000-plus years later.

Paul loved people. He believed in community. He traveled with friends, stayed with friends, prayed with friends, visited his friends, worked with his friends, as well as ministered alongside friends. He even sang in prison with his friends. He was a constant encouragement to the Christian community and they encouraged him in return.

Paul knew that fulfilling your God-given destiny was a team sport. This is why he surrounded himself with people like Barnabas, Titus, Silas, Luke, Priscilla, Aquilla, Lydia, Onesiphorus, Peter, Epapharoditus, John Mark, and so many more. In fact, in Romans 16, he mentions over 30 different names of personal friends and ministry partners that he loved and cared for. God wants this for you as well.

Thanks for getting your hands on this book and taking this journey with me. I believe it is going to deeply impact your life and help you become everything God has created you to be.

Let's jump in!

CHAPTER 1
DO YOU KNOW JACK?

A few months back, I was rummaging through our attic at home when I came across a shoe box full of hand-written notes from Junior High. I had forgotten all about them. Don't ask me why I decided to save these random notes… and don't ask me why they are organized alphabetically by name… but there they were.

Back before kids were texting and messaging their friends, they would pass notes to each other in school. Are any of you old enough (like me) to remember those days? If you had something to say, you wrote it on a note and passed it in the hall or when the teacher turned her back and wasn't looking. This is pre-emojis. Pre-cool abbreviations like BFF (Best Friends Forever), BBFEL (Best Friends for Everlasting Life), or BFFTLE (Best Friends For Totally Like Ever).

Most of these notes inside the dusty shoe box were from kids that I considered to be some of my BFFs, BBFELs, and BFFTLEs back in the day.

There's something special about remembering your childhood BFFs. Mine was Matt Hussong. What made Matt my best friend? We shared a ride to school together, each had a younger brother, and also went to the same church. That's about it: age proximity, the everlasting bond of sharing the rear-facing back seat of a '84 station wagon, and annoying little brothers.

I'm sure you can remember some of your best friends growing up. Although you may or may not still be connected today, those memories are special.

One of the greatest gifts that God gives you in life is friends. I cherish the friendships God has brought into my life. That includes ministry partners, employees, church friends, family, and especially my wife, Beth, who is my BFFTLE.

Friends in real life make living so much better. Proverbs says, "A friend loves at all times."[1] It is a privilege to have friends that truly love you, and whom you love back.

What makes up a genuine, long-lasting friendship?

The Bible is chock-full of friendship stories and good sound advice, such as:

- Quality trumps quantity when it comes to friendship. "Whoever walks with the wise becomes wise, but the companion of fools will suffer harm" (Proverbs 13:20).
- To have friends, you must be friendly yourself. "A man that hath friends must shew himself friendly" (Proverbs 18:24 KJV).
- Good friends aren't judgmental. "Do not speak evil against one another, brothers" (James 4:11).
- Friends practice forgiveness. "Bear with one another and, if anyone has a complaint against another, forgive each other; just as the Lord has forgiven you, so you also must forgive" (Colossians 3:13).
- Friends stay close in hard times. "A friend loves at all times" (Proverbs 17:17).
- Friends put up with your shortcomings and support you "Bear one another's burdens, and so

fulfill the law of Christ" (Galatians 6:2).
- Friends slow down and listen. "Know this, my beloved brothers: let every person be quick to hear, slow to speak, slow to anger" (James 1:19).
- Good friends leave a positive influence. "Do not be deceived: 'Bad company ruins good morals'" (1 Corinthians 15:33).
- Love will cover offenses between friends. "Whoever covers an offense seeks love, but he who repeats a matter separates close friends" (Proverbs 17:9).

That is just a small dose of the wisdom found in the Bible about friendship.

By the way, Matt is still one of my best friends today. We randomly call each other on our morning commute. We joke about conversions we had in the back of that station wagon. Our families hang out for game nights and take vacations together.

Why is it that, even from a young age, we want to belong, we want to be known, we want BFFs (or BBFELs or BFFTLEs) in our lives? The answer goes back to Genesis.

YOU WERE CREATED FOR COMMUNITY

Ishii Yuichi, is a thirty-seven year old father to over 25 families and a husband to over 600 women... but none of them are his real family members. Together with the 1,200 actors he employs at his company, he has played every part from stand-in father for a wedding, missing dad, long lost son, and even make-believe groom in his job as a companion for hire. For a fee, customers can find friends to pose with in happy

Instagram photos, an infant to impersonate a grandson, or a groom for a staged wedding.[2]

This seemingly strange industry, known as "rent-a-family", is trending in other countries as well. This forces us to ask the question: Why would someone go to the effort of actually renting a family?

This growing trend reflects an important truth. People rent families because we are created by God with a need for community. Everyone needs a place to belong.

The Bible is all about community. God chose the Israelites to be his people. "And I will walk among you and will be your God, and you shall be my people."[3] They lived together and worshiped him in community.

Following the death, resurrection, and ascension of Christ; God then instituted the church, the Body of Christ as a community. The Apostle Paul said, "Now you are the body of Christ and individually members of it."[4]

In the first two chapters of the Bible, we read the incredible story of creation. God created the land, the sea, the sky, the birds, the fish, the animals… and then He created man. When God breathed life into man, He came alive and enjoyed a relationship and fellowship with God. The Bible infers that God would come and talk with Adam in the cool of the day.

Shortly after God created Adam, a crisis arose. Some people think the first crisis had to do with the serpent and the forbidden fruit, but it happened before that. The first crisis in the Bible wasn't sin. It was loneliness.

> The first crisis in the Bible wasn't sin. It was loneliness.

God said, "It is not good that the man should be alone; I will make him a helper fit for him."[5] Adam was alone. The first human needed another human. God created us with a need for community. Although we are "fearfully and wonderfully made"[6], we are also deficient. We are deficient by design. We need others.

God said, "It is not good that the man should be alone." The original Hebrew uses the words *towb* or *tob*, meaning "pleasing" or "good" combined with *lo*, meaning "no" or "not." It also uses the Hebrew word for alone, taken from the root word *badad*, which Strong's Concordance defines as "to be separate, isolated" The original Hebrew indicates that God was not pleased that the man was isolated and on his own.[7]

God knew that Adam was alone and needed a relationship. He wasn't just referring to a divine relationship, either. Adam had already been enjoying a relationship with God before God said this. God was teaching an important lesson that I want you to hear right now as you hold this book in your hands.

You were created for community.

YOU + GOD + COMMUNITY

When I was about five years old, my parents converted a storage shed in our yard into a hair salon for my mom. My favorite part of my mom's little salon was the refrigerator where she kept soda and candy for her customers to purchase. I can definitely assure you that she ran a loss in the snack department thanks to my brother and I.

Along with the red cream soda and Hershey bars, I remember a brown, three-legged stool that mom had picked up somewhere to use in the salon.

Three-legged stools are pretty fascinating to study, actually. I bet you have never paused to consider that, have you?

Don't go.

Stick with me.

Did you know that it's impossible for a three-legged stool to wobble? It's true! (Knowing that fact alone is well worth the price of this book.)

Stools with four legs can – and often do – wobble. If the four legs are uneven, or if the floor isn't flat, the stool will wobble. It will rest first on one set of three legs, then tip to another. Stools with three legs, however, are solid..

Over the years, I've heard a lot of well-intentioned people say, "All I need is God." In one sense, that sounds spiritual and true, but it's actually unbiblical and false. God created you with a need for both divine relationship and human relationships.

You, God, and others are the three legs of the stool. You + God + a community of others complete the stool. And remember, a 3-legged stool is super sturdy. Take one of those legs away, and the stool is useless. When God or others are missing in your life, problems are sure to arise.

The New Testament emphasizes the value of community repeatedly. Did you know that the phrase "one another" occurs 100 times in the New Testament? Fifty-nine of those occurrences are specific commands teaching us how (and how not) to relate to each other.

Obedience to those commands is imperative. It forms the basis for all true Christian community, and has a direct impact on our witness to the world. Jesus said, "By this all people will know that you are my disciples, if you have love for one another."[8]

God created us with a need for one another and responsibilities toward one another. He created us to have friends in real life. This is not just a truth taught to us in the Bible, but it is also confirmed in research.

> God created us with a need for one another and responsibilities toward one another.

A popular Harvard study confirms this. "Good relationships keep us happier and healthier," Dr. Robert Waldinger, a psychiatrist and director of the Harvard Study of Adult Development, said in a popular TED Talk.

The ongoing Harvard study is considered one of the world's longest studies of adult life, having started in 1938 during the Great Depression.

"Our study has shown that the people who fared the best were the people who leaned into relationships, with family, with friends, with community," Waldinger said.

THE DOWNSIDE OF TECHNOLOGY

In our virtual world, it's easy to become relationally challenged. Stop and think about it. It's possible to go through much of your day without ever interacting with a single person.

Many of us do our banking online with no human contact. When we call the pharmacy, we are greeted by an automated system. Instead of talking to family on the phone, we send texts because they are faster and easier.

I remember before social media and texting when I would get 10 or 15 phone calls each day. Thanks to technology, we communicate in other ways. Now I only get 3 or 4 calls a day.

A few years back, Beth and I bought a car wash. Our oldest daughter, Luci, has special needs and loves anything that involves water. We bought the car wash with the intent that Luci would work there and we could employ other special needs kids and adults. I'm sharing this story because even at Luci's Car wash, a robot-like voice tells you when to pull in, when to place your car in park, and when to exit at the end of the wash.

Don't get me wrong. I love technology. My iPhone runs my life. However, we must beware of growing relationally challenged while growing more and more sophisticated and techy.

A Cornell study shows we have more connections on social media than in real life.[9] If that's the case – which it probably is – who are you leaning on? Who is helping you navigate the difficult decisions with your kids? Whose shoulder are you crying on? Who are you laughing with?

Matthew Brashears, a Cornell University sociologist, surveyed more than 2,000 adults and found that from 1985 to 2010, the number of close friends dropped. This was 12 years ago — how bad is it now? Many people count their connections on social media as friends, but when pushed, admit they really aren't friends, only connections.

The virtual world improves our lives, makes organizations run efficiently, and creates incredible opportunities for ministry. However, technology has also created relationally challenged individuals. Too many people are high tech and low touch... and this is a serious problem. You were created for community. You need relationships.

> Too many people are high tech and low touch...
> and this is a serious problem.

Les and Leslie Parrott said, "Neglecting your longing for relationships by claiming to be above it is as foolish as pretending you can live without food." That may seem a little far fetched. Are relationships really that important? Can they affect me like living without food? Before we answer that question, let's hit pause.

I love food. Beth and I are definitely what you would term foodies.

Let me share a recent crisis in my own life. (Crisis is probably extreme, but keep reading. I'll explain.) I'm now at the age where I go to the doctor for an annual checkup and blood work. Come to find out, yours truly has high cholesterol. I join the nearly 40% of other American adults dealing with this issue.

This guy who loves to eat (especially dessert) has changed his diet and is now attempting to eat clean. I hope that by the time you read this I'm still good at the table. Ask me the next time we talk.

Okay, let's return from that rabbit trail and get back to the topic at hand.

Can neglecting relationships really affect your health like living without food? Absolutely!

Scientists are finding that our relationships with others do have significant effects on our health. Whether with family, friends, neighbors, or others; social connections can influence our biology and well-being. Wide-ranging research suggests real life friendships are linked to a longer life. In contrast, loneliness and social isolation are linked to poorer health, depression, and increased risk of early death.[10]

There, you've got it.

So… what do you do? How do you avoid becoming relationally challenged? How do you build a real community in a virtual world?

SURFACE-LEVEL FRIENDS VS REAL LIFE FRIENDS

This is the most connected age in history. We look into people's lives across the world from our phones and computer screens every day, yet we can't seem to find a true, close friend in our own backyard. This is why it's important to understand the difference between surface-level friends and real life friends.

Surface-level friends are just that. People you know on the surface and in return they know you the same way. It stops at the surface and goes no deeper than that.

Surface-level friends are people you meet at church, at the baseball diamond, at work, on social media, or they are a friend of someone you know. They are possibly available to chat when you see a little green dot next to their name on your phone. You might squeeze in a 60-second conversation every once in a while if you meet in the church hallway or in line at the concession stand. These people are interesting, fun, and can even add some level of value to your life.

The greatest part about surface-level friends is they take zero effort. The conversations normally go no deeper than "Where did you say you went on vacation last summer?" or "How has your mom been feeling?" You run into each other in various places like church, the gym, or your kid's school and make conversation. You may really enjoy each other. It's just that one or both of you doesn't have the time or desire to go any further than surface-level. It can also be very lonely to know a lot of people who are just surface-level friends.

Real life friends, on the other hand, are entirely different. You have history with this person. There has been significant time invested. You know this person well and they know you well. (And despite this, they like you anyway!)

You can call a real friend at 2:00 AM and you know they will answer their phone. This friend will stop everything for you. Sometimes they know you better than you know yourself. With gentle honesty, real life friends are there to guide and support you. They share your laughter and your tears. They aren't jealous when something great happens to you. When you hit a patch of turbulence in your life, real life friends jump into the cockpit with you and help you pilot your way out.

Avoid becoming relationally challenged by understanding the difference between surface-level friends and real life ones.

DON'T OBSESS OVER THE NUMBERS

Eighteen years ago, Beth and I started a non-profit organization named KidzMatter to serve those who minister to kids and families in the church. If you are reading this book, there's a good chance that you have been impacted in one way or another by this ministry. You subscribe to KidzMatter Magazine, you attend The KidzMatter Conference (formally called KidzMatter MegaCon), you are a graduate of Kidmin Academy, you are a part of our I Love Kidmin Facebook community, or you utilize the downloadable resources at KidzMatter.com.

I speak for Beth in saying that one of our favorite parts of leading KidzMatter is seeing what happens when ministry leaders realize they aren't alone. It's a breath of fresh air and wind behind their sails.

Every year, we survey our Kidmin Academy graduates and ask them a variety of questions to help us improve this 12-month diploma program. One question we ask is, "What part of Kidmin Academy made the biggest impact in your life?"

You would think we would hear about a favorite faculty member or a module that helped them tackle a big problem they have been facing in their church. However, 8 out of 10 graduates tell us that the biggest impact was found within the community of students. They were deeply impacted by the relationships that were formed.

There is power in surrounding yourself with a large number of people. However, don't take the bait of obsessing over the numbers.

Being obsessed with how many friends and connections you have is a dangerous trap that you've got to resist at all costs. It will keep you from the most important things. It distracts from your life. And it's bad for your spiritual, emotional, and mental health.

It's not a race to see who has the most friends on Facebook. It's not a battle for the most followers, subscribers, or views.

It's not about the quantity… it's about the quality.

I wonder if in the attempt to connect with as many people as humanly possible, we are hurting ourselves. Is it really better to interact with more people than fewer people? This leads to our next question.

DO YOU KNOW JACK?

Here's the thing if we are honest… we really know hardly anyone. I maxed out the number of friends Facebook allows a person to have (which is 5,000) several years ago. At the time of this writing, there are nearly 30,000 members of our Facebook community. I share this to make this point: I have a lot of friends out there… but how many of them do I really know?

> Here's the thing if we are honest...
> we really know hardly anyone.

Our virtual world forces upon us a feeling of intimacy and closeness that doesn't actually exist.

You know that feeling you get when you're watching a TV show, or someone's stories or reels, and you just know that you would get along really well with that person in real life? You know you'd be the best of friends. The more you absorb their content, the more connected you feel to that person. Even though you have never met them in real life, you are convinced that you'd be tight. In all actuality, it's nothing more than a one-sided relationship (but you can't help it).

This concept is known as a parasocial relationship. This phrase was coined in 1956 by Donald Horton and R. Richard Wohl to describe the way mass media users acted like they were in a typical relationship with a media figure, such as feeling as though they are friends with a radio personality or a TV character. While this type of one-sided relationship existed long before the invention of TV and radio, the growing role of social media has brought this concept into prominence. So much so, it's become overwhelmingly common for people to describe any relationship on social media as parasocial.

The virtual world we live in only encourages this. The potential to form parasocial relationships is weaved into the DNA of places like Facebook, Snapchat, TikTok, Instagram, and YouTube. You become friends or a follower or a subscriber of someone who then shares their thoughts "directly to you".

And that is our virtual world. A parasocial world that, for so many, is getting in the way of true community.

Researchers polled 3,053 adults and found their obsession with socializing online made many less likely to go out and meet people. In fact, 6 in 10 adults admit they spent less time catching up with friends since the world became more digital.

In addition to this, 55% of those polled believe social media has made relationships with their friends "more superficial". It could be the reason why a third said they wished they had a greater number of close friends.[11]

Are you satisfied with the number of close friends you have? How well do you know them? It's imperative that we value real friends and spend time deepening those relationships.

Jonathan Sawyer is one of the most anointed worship leaders I know. That's why Beth and I invite him to lead worship each year at The KidzMatter Conference... but I've never met his kids.

Justin Eggar is one of my closest advisors at Frank Insurance Management... but our families have never spent time together.

Ken Ham from Answers in Genesis and I wrote a book together... but I have never met his wife or kids.

Here's my point. I consider these people (and so many others) to be good friends. They are a gift and a treasure. I'm also thankful for my surface-level friends (many of which social media has brought into my life.) But when I look at my surface-level friends, I know almost nothing about them.

Is that what we really want? Is that what's best for us? Spending so much time making as many surface-level friends as possible, potentially at the expense of our cherished relationships with real life friends?

Do you really know Jack?

EVERYONE DOES BETTER WITH A COACH

"Everyone needs a coach." These are the words Bill Gates used to open a TED Talk. He went on to say, "We all need people that give us feedback. That's how we improve." One of the points that he highlights in the talk – and the one characteristic common to all high performing individuals, from executives to athletes – is the fact that they all have a coach.

Yet, surprisingly so many people (especially ministry people) don't have a coach. Maybe it's because they are too proud... or too embarrassed... or too afraid of what people will think if they ask for a coach.

In my experience working with both ministry and marketplace leaders, those who seek coaching aren't the ones with something wrong with them. They are the ones that move further, faster.

> In my experience working with both ministry and marketplace leaders, those who seek coaching aren't the ones with something wrong with them. They are the ones that move further, faster.

As we consider the fact that we need real community in a virtual world, where do we look for coaching and help?

We start in God's Word.

Over the course of this book, we will explore the life and ministry of the Apostle Paul. We will discover some key points to making friends in real life and building real community in this virtual world.

WHEN YOUR GREATEST ENEMIES BECOME YOUR GREATEST FRIENDS

Except for Jesus, Paul is considered the most significant influential spiritual contributor to the Christian faith. He wrote 13 of the 27 books of the New Testament. His writing and preaching helped the early church and are an encouragement to us today. How did it all begin?

The early church faced an extremely difficult challenge. Persecutors like Paul (who went by the name of Saul at that time) attacked believers, put them in jail, and had them killed.

Saul had gained a reputation as the ringleader of the movement to make Christianity extinct. A devout Hellenistic Jew, of the tribe of Benjamin, born in Tarsus of Cilicia; Saul was a member of the Pharisees and was taught by none other than Gamaliel, an influential Pharisee and an expert of the law. Saul did not agree with his teacher, Gamaliel, on how the Christians should be dealt with, however. Rather, he sought the arrest, trial, conviction, and punishment (with imprisonment the norm and death the ideal) of those in Jerusalem. His career as a persecutor of Christians seems to have begun with Stephen, but it quickly spread to all of the Christians in Jerusalem.

But Jesus changed Saul's plans. Isn't it something how He does that?

Saul obtained permission from the high priest to go to Damascus. He was hoping to find and arrest Christians who had fled his persecution. So intent was he on "opposing the name of Jesus of Nazareth" that in "raging fury," he breathed "threats and murder against the disciples of the Lord." This was a man who truly hated Christ and all who were associated with Him.

While on the way, a bright light shone on Saul, causing his entire party to fall to the ground.

Whenever I get to this point in the story, I always visualize a movie scene where a criminal is running the street in the dark of night and a helicopter shines the brightest searchlight ever down to stop him in his tracks. I know it wasn't quite like that, but it was dramatic for sure.

After seeing the great light, Paul fell to the ground and heard Jesus' voice asking why he was persecuting Him. He was blinded by the light. The voice then told him what to do. His companions led him to Damascus.

In the meantime, the Lord commanded a believer named Ananias to meet Saul and minister to him. Despite his fear, Ananias obeyed.

Saul, soon to be known as Paul, regained his sight, and began his ministry. He was then baptized. You can read the whole story in Acts 9.

Paul preached across the Roman Empire, over 10,000 miles, and even appeared before Caesar. Paul proclaimed the Gospel "to the Gentiles and their kings and to the people of Israel."[12]

His greatest enemies became his greatest friends in real life.

YOUR LIFE WAS DESIGNED TO BE A COMMUNITY PROJECT

Paul wrote 13 letters to the church. These are in the Bible today and we are discussing them right now in this book... so in one sense he continues to proclaim Jesus' name around the world. In his writings, we see his deep love for Christ and the church. He gave his life to building community. Many of his letters to the churches begin and end with tributes to his friends; those who ministered to him, supported him, prayed for him, and loved him.

I want to highlight one of the letters that Paul wrote to the early church. It's found in Colossians 2. Read these words as if you were peeking over Paul's shoulder as he wrote them:

> "For I want you to know how great a struggle I have for you and for those at Laodicea and for all who have not seen me face to face, that their hearts may be encouraged, *being knit together in love*, to reach all the riches of full assurance of understanding and the knowledge of God's mystery, which is Christ, in whom are hidden all the treasures of wisdom and knowledge. I say this in order that no one may delude you with plausible arguments. For though I am absent in body, yet I am with you in spirit, rejoicing to see your good order and the firmness of your faith in Christ. Therefore, as you received Christ Jesus the Lord, so walk in Him, rooted and built up in Him and established in the faith, just as you were taught, abounding in thanksgiving"[13] (emphasis mine).

In this letter to the community in Colosse, Paul expressed among other things his desire that they be knit together in love.

I love that imagery. "Knit together in love."

The word "knit," or "knit together," simply means to unite. It really is a beautiful picture of the body of Christ, all of us being knit together in an indivisible kind of oneness. Your body is a combination of billions of cells, all knit together. You can't pick any one of them apart, because they blend indiscriminately together. This is what God wants for the Christian community.

We need each other. We need to trust, rely on, and depend upon other believers. God gave us each other to walk alongside, encourage, and challenge us in the faith.

The writer of Hebrews says, "And let us consider how to stir up one another to love and good works, not neglecting to meet together, as is the habit of some, but encouraging one another, and all the more as you see the Day drawing near."[14]

Paul Tripp says:

> "We weren't created to be independent, autonomous, or self-sufficient. We were made to live in a humble, worshipful, and loving dependency upon God and in a loving and humble interdependency with others. Our lives were designed to be community projects. Yet, the foolishness of sin tells us that we have all that we need within ourselves. So we settle for relationships that never go beneath the casual. We defend ourselves when the people around us point out a weakness or a wrong. We hold our struggles within, not taking advantage of the resources God has given us."[15]

FRIENDS IN REAL LIFE

We live in a growing virtual world. Others might tell you that you can do life on your own and you don't need real community. However, God says that you simply can't function without others. Everybody has a longing for belonging because God made us for relationships. Don't spend so much time making friends online that you risk disconnecting with the real life friends who need you offline.

> ▶ *Don't spend so much time making friends online that you risk disconnecting with the real life friends who need you offline.*

You need a BFF or BBFEL or BFFTLE.
You are made for community.

▶ IN REAL LIFE
PROTECTING YOUR REAL LIFE FRIENDS

We all need real life friends. Solomon said, "Oil and perfume make the heart glad, and the sweetness of a friend comes from his earnest counsel."[16] Real life friends are a treasure... and treasures should be protected.

1. Spend time together.
Friendships require staying connected and spending time together. Do your best to check in with texts and phone calls, and try to schedule some time just to hang out and talk. Proverbs says, "Spend time with the wise and you will become wise."[17]

2. Be honest.
Superficial relationships fizzle over time. To have a lasting friendship, you have to be honest with each other. A real life friend won't tell you what you want to hear, but what you need to hear. "Better is open rebuke than hidden love. Faithful are the wounds of a friend; profuse are the kisses of an enemy."[18]

3. Be kind.
Go out of your way to be kind and to practice encouragement. A little encouragement goes a long way! "A word fitly spoken is like apples of gold in a setting of silver. Like a gold ring or an ornament of gold is a wise reprover to a listening ear."[19]

4. Listen more than you talk.
The average person has an eight-second attention span.[20] With electronic distractions competing for your time and a load of responsibilities at home and work; it makes listening attentively to a friend pretty difficult. Yet, we all know it's

hugely important. James said, "let every person be quick to hear, slow to speak."[21]

5. Admit when you're wrong.
No one is perfect. You are going to mess up at times, but when you do, set your pride aside and say you are sorry. Apologizing is part of staying humble, and humility is a character quality God holds in high esteem. "Humble yourselves before the Lord, and he will exalt you."[22]

Don't underestimate the importance of protecting your friendships. Australian nurse Bronnie Ware listed "not maintaining friendships" as one of people's biggest death-bed regrets.[23] Cultivating real life friendships is critical in becoming the person God wants you to be.

CHAPTER 2
PROACTIVELY JOINING GOD AT WORK

An elderly lady was known all around town for her Christian faith and her boldness in proclaiming it. She was known to stand on her front porch and shout "Praise the Lord!" so loud that everyone around the block could hear. Next door to her lived an atheist who would get so angry at her fits of praise that he would shout, "There ain't no Lord!"

This lady came into some hard times and she prayed for God to send her some help. She stood on her porch and shouted. "Praise God! I need some food. I am having a hard time! Please Lord, send me some groceries." The next morning the lady went out on her porch and saw two large bags of groceries. She started shouting "Praise the Lord! God answered my prayer!"

Right then, the neighbor jumped from behind the bush and said, "Aha! I told you there was no God. I bought those groceries for you myself. They didn't come from God." The lady started jumping up and down, clapping her hands and shouting, "Praise the Lord! He not only heard my prayer and sent groceries, but He made the devil pay for them!"

I don't know how true that story is, but I do know that prayer is powerful. Would you agree? Jesus promised, "Whatever you ask in prayer, you will receive, if you have faith."[1] When a community comes together to pray, the doors of heaven open.

> When a community comes together to pray, the doors of heaven open.

We see this with the early church. They were a praying community. The church started at a prayer meeting on the Day of Pentecost and the disciples continued to pray as they went on their way sharing the good news of Jesus around the world.

This really shouldn't surprise us. The leaders of the early church had gone to Jesus earlier and asked Him to teach them to pray which He did. He then instructed them to teach others what He had taught them. From Jesus, to the disciples, to the first-century Christians, and down through the years to us; the church has taught and practiced prayer.

And when prayer is taught and practiced, the results are amazing.

THE CHURCH IS BORN

Before Jesus ascended into heaven, He instructed His disciples to not leave Jerusalem. He had nothing else for them to do other than to wait for the promise of the Father. This promise was the Old Testament promise spoken of by the prophet Joel that believers would be baptized with the Holy Ghost.

> "And while staying with them He ordered them not to depart from Jerusalem, but to wait for the promise of the Father, which, He said, 'you heard from me; for John baptized with water, but you will be baptized

with the Holy Spirit not many days from now. But you will receive power when the Holy Spirit has come upon you, and you will be my witnesses in Jerusalem and in all Judea and Samaria, and to the end of the earth.'"[2]

Jesus knew that they could do nothing effectively for the Kingdom of God until the Holy Spirit came. They had three and one-half years of theological training and hands-on coaching by Jesus Himself. They had witnessed lives changed and amazing miracles performed. They knew Jesus closely and intimately. Yet, they had to wait.

They followed the instructions:

> "They went up to the upper room, where they were staying, Peter and John and James and Andrew, Philip and Thomas, Bartholomew and Matthew, James the son of Alphaeus and Simon the Zealot and Judas the son of James. All these with one accord were devoting themselves to prayer, together with the women and Mary the mother of Jesus, and his brothers."[3]

They didn't rush off to become world changers. They listened, obeyed, and waited. They didn't forget the sermon right after they heard it like I often do. They actually followed Jesus' instructions even though He was no longer physically with them.

There were about 120 of them waiting in that upper room. It must have been a big room to hold all of those people. This included the eleven disciples (the twelve minus Judas); along with Mary, the mother of Jesus, the brothers of Jesus (such as James and Jude), the women who followed Jesus, and others.

The Bible says they were together in one accord devoted to prayer.

When I was a kid, my dad had a great joke that I still remember. Here it is:

What kind of car did the disciples drive? A Honda. The Bible says they were all in one Accord.

I told you my jokes were lame. I may have come by it naturally.

While in the upper room they were in one accord. They were unified in their hearts and minds. Interestingly, when we saw the disciples earlier in the Gospels, it seemed that they always fought and argued. What changed? Peter still had the history of denying the Lord. James and his brother, John, were still "the sons of thunder." Matthew was still a tax collector. Simon was still a zealot. Their differences were still there, but the resurrected Jesus in their hearts was greater than any difference.

Luke records the first activity of the disciples once in the upper room. They joined together in prayer and supplication. Supplication is a sense of desperation and earnestness in prayer.

What happened next was nothing short of incredible. It was the Day of Pentecost. Thousands of Jews had gathered to celebrate it.

> "When the day of Pentecost arrived, they were all together in one place. And suddenly there came from heaven a sound like a mighty rushing wind, and it filled the entire house where they were sitting. And divided tongues as of fire appeared to them and rested on each one of them. And they were all filled with the Holy Spirit and began to speak in other tongues as the Spirit gave them utterance."[4]

This was a Pentecost like none other. The disciples expected to participate in the festivities, but their plans changed. The Holy Spirit came to form the church!

On the Old Testament Day of Pentecost, God gave the Law. On the New Testament Day of Pentecost, God gave the gift of the Holy Spirit. Right then and there, the disciples were baptized and filled with the Holy Spirit.

What exactly happened on the Day of Pentecost? People a lot smarter than me have debated it over and over. There is one thing we know for sure. On that day, the church was born and the people were empowered as never before. Before, they had been afraid and cowardly. Now, they had a new boldness that no one could fathom followed by an outpouring of God's blessings.

On the first Sunday, 3,000 people came to faith in Jesus Christ. At their second public gathering, over 5,000 were added to the church. Historians tell us that within 6 months of Pentecost, there were over 100,000 new Christians in the city of Jerusalem.

When you realize the magnitude of what happened through this small group of people, it boggles the mind. It forces you to ask: What was it about this community that enabled them to accomplish so much in such little time? They were nothing more than a group of nobodies. Nobody knew their names. Nobody knew their families. They had few (if any) followers. They had no platform. Yet, history records that they were used by God to literally turn the world upside down.

> What was it about this community that enabled them to accomplish so much in such little time? They were nothing more than a group of nobodies.

These men and women were an unlikely group of people, but they had a faith that produced obedience. They had a passion that produced unity. They had a desperation that produced prayer. They had the Spirit of the living God that produced power.[5]

PETITION, PROTEST, OR PRAYER?

The book of Acts provides a recorded history of the role that prayer played in the early Christian community. There are around 30 references to prayer in the book of Acts alone. This is more than any other book in the New Testament.

Prayer goes before almost every major event of the early church.

Tim Barnett says,

> "Prayer precedes almost every major event of the early church. Prayer precedes the filling of the Holy Spirit, multiple healings, bold preaching, and comfort for persecuted believers."[6]

Prayer also preceded numerous miracles, like the one I am about to share with you. In Acts 12, the Christian community was in crisis. Persecution began to strike through Herod Agrippa I. This is the grandson of Herod the Great (who attempted to put Jesus to death at the time of His birth.) When you study history, you'll find that there was never a family more at animosity toward God than this.

Up to this point the persecution against the church had been largely from the religious leaders. Now it has moved into the realm of the government. Persecution swung from religion to politics.

Luke records that Herod had taken captive a number of the early Christians. He killed James and proceeded to imprison Peter with the intent of killing him as well.

Peter's life would miraculously be saved. I am sure there were many who asked, "Why would James be put to death and Peter allowed to live? Why would God do that?"

How many times have I asked myself the same question, "Why would God do that?" Why would God allow a young mother to die of cancer, while others survive? Why would God allow such a good person to go through miscarriage after miscarriage? The answer is the sovereign will of God. Life and death are ultimately in His hands. It is God's world, not yours. It's His ministry, not yours. It is His family, not yours.

Herod had Peter thrown into jail and he proceeded to put four squads of four soldiers each to guard him. I would say that he suspected someone would try to free Peter. He was planning a public lynching after Passover.

The church in Jerusalem didn't respond with a petition or a protest, but with a prayer meeting. While Peter was in prison, "earnest prayer for him was made to God by the church."[7] They were purposefully praying that Peter would be set free.

> The church in Jerusalem didn't respond with a petition or a protest, but with a prayer meeting.

At the same time the community was praying for Peter, an angel of the Lord helped him escape from prison. I love how God answers this prayer – down to the very details.

Peter, the night before his planned execution, enjoyed a good sleep between two soldiers. How could he sleep between two soldiers? And how could he be sleeping so well?

Peter didn't fight insomnia. Remember that he also went to sleep in the Garden of Gethsemane. Sleep came easy for him. (That is one thing that Peter and I have in common. The ability to sleep about anywhere and anytime!) Isn't it great that Peter was so confident that God could deliver him that he was able to sleep between two soldiers?

An angel appeared in the prison cell and a bright light shined, but no one woke up — not even Peter. Peter was sleeping so well that the angel literally had to hit him on his side to wake him up. The chains fell to the ground, which would have created a loud sound, but the soldiers didn't notice! They passed the guards and all the prison doors opened for him. He was free.

Amazed, he went straight to Mary's house, the Mary who was John Mark's mother. She was apparently a woman of wealth and had a house large enough for the church to meet there. Her house was packed with praying friends.

By the way, the church at this time did not have church buildings. For nearly 300 years Christians were "one of the few religious groups at the time that did not make use of some sort of sacred buildings or structures."[8]

Actually, a church building is not the church at all. Your church building might be on the corner of 10th and Main, but that is not the church. The church is the community of believers. In the beginning, the church never met in public buildings because they didn't have any. They met in their homes.

When Peter knocked on the door, a young woman named Rhoda came to see who it was. The Bible says she was listening to the knock on the door. These were days of persecution. It was important to know who was knocking. When she recognized Peter's voice, she was so excited to tell everyone he was there that she forgot to open the door and left him standing in the street.

Instead of believing her, they dismissed her as being out of her mind. They thought it was Peter's spirit. In other words, they thought he had been killed by Herod and it was his dead spirit visiting.

Peter kept on knocking, which is just like Peter. Nobody opened the gate because they didn't believe their prayers had been answered. They were all inside arguing whether it was Peter or whether it was his spirit. Peter wanted in and I'm sure was about ready to knock the gate down!

When they finally responded to Peter's knocking at the gate, they were astounded to see it was indeed Peter, not his spirit, standing before them. The people made such a commotion that Peter had to motion for them to keep quiet, so he could tell them how God had rescued him.

It is interesting that while the church was praying for Peter to be delivered... he was delivered. And when it happened, they didn't believe it. They couldn't believe that their prayers had been answered.

How often do we do the same thing? It is so good to know that the early church struggled with much of the same stuff we do. How often do we pray and when the answer finally comes we get excited and talk about it like we are really surprised? And if we are honest – we really are surprised. We didn't expect God to answer, and yet He did.

Jesus said, "For where two or three are gathered in my name, there am I among them."[9] When you study the book of Acts and the early church, you don't see a group of people sitting around the Bible taking prayer requests followed by that awkward silence that we have all experienced at prayer request time.

They didn't just pray before a meal or with a grocery-list of wants. Prayer was action. It was proactively joining God at work.

▶ Prayer was action. It was proactively joining God at work.

50,000 ANSWERED PRAYERS

George Mueller is by far one of my heroes of the faith. He is considered one the greatest men of prayer since the days of the New Testament. He lived nearly the entire nineteenth century, two-thirds of it in Bristol, England. He led four far-reaching and influential ministries, but we know him best today for his orphanages.

During a time in England when most orphans lived in miserable workhouses or on the streets, like in Charles Dickens's Oliver Twist; Mueller took them in, fed them, clothed them, and educated them. Through his orphanage in Bristol, George cared for as many as 2,000 orphans at a time — more than 10,000 in his lifetime. Yet he never made the needs of his ministries known to anyone except to God in prayer. Only through his annual reports did people learn after the fact what the needs had been during the previous year and how God had provided.

George Mueller had over 50,000 specific recorded answers to prayers in his journals, 30,000 of which he said were answered the same day or the same hour that he prayed them. Think of it: that's 500 definite answers to prayer each year – more than one per day – every single day for 60 years! God funneled over half a billion dollars (in today's dollars) through his hands in answer to prayer.[10]

I could spend an entire chapter sharing stories of how God answered his prayers. I'll share one of my favorites.

"The children are dressed and ready for school. But there is no food for them to eat," the housemother of the orphanage informed George Mueller. George asked her to take the 300 children into the dining room and have them sit at the tables. He thanked God for the food and waited. George knew God would provide food for the children as He always did. Within minutes, a baker knocked on the door. "Mr. Mueller," he said, "last night I could not sleep. Somehow I knew that you would need bread this morning. I got up and baked three batches for you. I will bring it in."

Soon, there was another knock at the door. It was the milkman. His cart had broken down in front of the orphanage. The milk would spoil by the time the wheel was fixed. He asked George if he could use some free milk. George smiled as the milkman brought in ten large cans of milk. It was just enough for the 300 thirsty children.[11]

It has been over 180 years since George Mueller took in his first orphan. His legacy continues today as Christians around the world are inspired by his faith to depend on God and to join Him at work in prayer.

THE BENEFITS OF PRAYING TOGETHER

It's easy to think of prayer as a solitary endeavor, a private conversation between God and yourself. When most people think about prayer, they imagine someone kneeling in front of their bed, hands clasped together and eyes closed. While there is nothing wrong with praying by yourself (in fact, it's hugely important), praying with a community of others is crucial.

I just shared some incredible stories of answered prayer. Perhaps you have experienced a similar story personally or seen answered prayer in the life of someone you know.

A baby born entirely too premature fights and makes it. A teenager that should have died in a serious car accident is healed. A college student who has walked away from the Lord returns to her faith. A church that is struggling to stay afloat experiences growth after some of its members began gathering to pray.

There is power when people pray together. Psalm promises, "The LORD is near to all who call on him, to all who call on him in truth."[12] We amplify the power of prayer when we pray together.

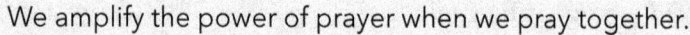 We amplify the power of prayer when we pray together.

1. PRAYING TOGETHER BRINGS GOD'S PRESENCE.

When the early church prayed together, they were filled with the Holy Spirit and they began to know God's presence in a new way. Paul said, "Because of Christ and our faith in Him, we can now come boldly and confidently into God's presence."[13]

My girls are still young enough that they like a good game of hide and seek from time to time. You know how it works. Someone hides and someone searches.

When I first started as a children's pastor, we played a game at church camp for several years that I shutter to even tell you about. It was a camp-wide game of hide and seek that we called Safari. We waited until it got dark and all the adults would go and hide. After about 15 minutes, the kids were released to run around the camp and find the adults. In hindsight, the idea of letting eight and ten-year-old kids loose in the darkness of night with no adult supervision was not the best of ideas. Anyway, one year I decided to hide on the top of the dining hall with one of our volunteers, Jeremy. It seemed like the perfect hideout. The good news is that not one kid found us. The bad news was we couldn't get down… literally.

I'll spare you the details. I'll just say that it was traumatic enough that we never played Safari again. That game of hide and seek came to a sudden and abrupt end!

I recently stumbled upon a verse in the Bible that astounded me. An Old Testament prophet boldly told King Asa, "The eyes of the Lord *search the whole earth* in order to strengthen those whose hearts are fully committed to Him"[14] (emphasis mine).

How awesome is that? God is seeking. He's not aimlessly seeking. He's searching for those who are reaching out to Him so He can bring them into His presence.

When we pray together we are essentially entering God's presence together. David wrote, "Oh, magnify the LORD with me, and let us exalt His name together!"[15] As we reach out to Him, His presence strengthens us and helps us exactly where we need it the most.

2. PRAYING TOGETHER BRINGS MORE ANSWERED PRAYERS.

Jesus said, "If two of you agree on earth about anything they ask, it will be done for them by my Father in heaven. For where two or three are gathered in my name, there am I among them."[16] There is power in engaging with others in prayer!

In the Old Testament, we learn a principle about the power of agreement. "Five of you shall chase a hundred, and a hundred of you shall chase ten thousand, and your enemies shall fall before you."[17] Go back and read that verse one more time. Being in agreement is the difference between one defeating twenty and one defeating a hundred. Some of the greatest battles in life are won when a community agrees together in prayer.

When we pray together, we each have a unique way of praying. I have friends who love to pray through song and worship. Others love to personalize the Scripture in prayer. Some enjoy simply being quiet and listening for the voice of God. Others have such empathy for others that they know exactly what to pray for and when. Every prayer in a community brings a different voice to the need.

> Every prayer in a community brings a different voice to the need.

There is power when God's people pray together. This doesn't mean that God isn't there when you're alone, it just reminds you that there is special power when we come together because your prayers are multiplied. The more people who are praying together means that collectively more prayers are being prayed.

3. PRAYING TOGETHER BRINGS UNITY.

John 17 is one of the most remarkable chapters in the Scriptures. It is the longest prayer recorded in the Bible, although it would only take you about three minutes to read.

Martin Luther loved John 17. "This is truly, beyond measure, a warm and hearty prayer. He opens the depths of His heart, both in reference to us and to His Father, and He pours them all out. It sounds so honest, so simple. It is so deep, so rich, so wide. No one can fathom it."

This is the prayer that John Knox read over and over in his lifetime. When he was on his deathbed, his wife asked him, "Where do you want me to read?" He replied. "Read where I first put my anchor down, in the seventeenth chapter of John."

In His prayer, Jesus said:

> "The same glory you gave me, I gave them,
> So they'll be as unified and together as we are—
> *I in them and you in me.*
> Then they'll be mature in this oneness,
> And give the godless world evidence
> That you've sent me and loved them
> In the same way you've loved me"[18] (emphasis mine).

How incredible! Only the Holy Spirit can accomplish this. The unity that exists between the Father and the Son is the unity that is to exist between you and Jesus Himself. Praying as a community brings the unity that Jesus Himself prayed for.

As a young pastor, I used to pray on Saturday mornings with a man in my church named Andy. Andy has a good number of years on me. We served in the bus ministry together. On Saturday mornings, we would meet at the church to pray. I can remember hearing Andy pray for the 40 or 50 kids on his bus route by name. He wasn't praying from a printed roster. The names of the kids were on his heart. Our hearts were unified as we prayed together.

It's amazing how praying together for others draws us closer in our relationships. As I write this, I am praying with hundreds of others for a friend named Matt. Matt is my age, has a beautiful wife and children, and was recently diagnosed with stage 4 colon and liver cancer. As a community of friends, we are growing closer together as we pray for a miracle.

4. PRAYING TOGETHER SHOWS YOU LOVE OTHERS.

Praying for someone is one of the best ways to show that you love them. As a pastor, I have asked a lot of people over the years if I can pray for them. Not one person that I can remember has ever told me no. Praying for someone is a loving gift that we can give that costs us nothing.

Paul said, "Carry each other's burdens, and in this way you will fulfill the law of Christ.[19]" People around you are carrying so many burdens with them every day. God wants you to share their burdens.

This is a simple command to obey. Look for someone with a burden and help them with it. It's really that easy. It doesn't require a program to pull it off. Just look for a burden to carry and carry it. Praying for someone is a powerful way to do this.

> Look for someone with a burden and help them with it. It's really that easy. It doesn't require a program to pull it off.

Several years ago Beth and I woke up in the middle of the night to someone pounding on our front door. We were both in such a deep sleep that like Peter at Mary's house, the pounding went on and on until we finally got up and answered the door. It had been raining hard outside and Beth's parents, who lived across the street, had a flood in their basement and needed our help.

Jesus said that consistent prayer is just like that. He said it's like pounding on your friend's door in the middle of the night until they finally get up to see what you need. You just keep at it until you get an answer.[20]

If you're anything like me, it's easy to commit to praying for someone and then totally forget about it as you go through the busyness of life. But how powerful it is when you actually remember to pray for them and join them in taking the burden of their heart before the presence of the Lord. When you do this, you show that you care enough to step into their struggle and genuinely love them.

You can be part of the help that God might choose to send to someone else in your life because you are willing to carry their burden and pray together.

5. PRAYING TOGETHER BRINGS STRENGTH.

During their wilderness march, the Israelites were facing an unprovoked attack by the Amalekites. Amalek was a descendent of Esau and they had become fierce enemies of Israel. They killed for sport and were on the attack against God's people. In response, Moses called Joshua to lead the armies of Israel into battle and to defend the nation against the attack from Amalek.

Moses told them that as Joshua led the people in battle, he would go to the top of the hill and hold out the staff of the Lord over them. As long as Moses' hands were up in the air, the Israelites were winning, but when his arms got tired, the enemy began to overtake them. The fate of Israel in battle was literally in the hands of Moses! His arms grew tired so Aaron and Hur came and held up his hands – one on one side, and one on the other.

What happened next? A miracle. Even though all odds were stacked against them, the people of Israel defeated this strong enemy.

The battle against the Amalekites wasn't fought on a battlefield. It was fought on a mountaintop. It was won by prayer. The victory didn't come as a result of Israel's fighting ability. This was their very first battle. It was won by Moses, Aaron, and Hur on the top of the mountain. Had they not done the work in prayer, Israel would have been defeated and history would have forever been changed. The work of prayer always outlasts our lifetime and changes history. Your prayers make a difference in your children and generations after them.

> The work of prayer always outlasts our lifetime and changes history.

You can lift your hands and your heart before the Lord today. He will give you the strength to do what seems to be impossible. Like Israel, you might be facing a battle you have never faced before. Even if you feel outnumbered or too tired to keep going, victory can be yours as you battle with others in prayer.

The Bible says, "Two are better than one, because they have a good reward for their toil. For if they fall, one will lift up his fellow. But woe to him who is alone when he falls and has not another to lift him up!"[21]

When you pray together, it reminds you that there are real people in your corner cheering you on and supporting you. Choose to start surrounding yourself with a like-minded community who will partner with you in prayer.

PRAYER MAKES A POWERFUL DIFFERENCE

There is power when a community comes together to pray. In prayer, we experience God's presence, healing, forgiveness, hope, and victory.

When we pray with others, God also releases His grace

and power into their lives. After encouraging the church to "pray for each other," James goes on to say, "The prayer of a righteous person has great power as it is working."[22] Prayer makes a powerful difference in the lives of the people we pray with.

R.A. Torrey wrote, "Prayer is the key that unlocks all the storehouses of God's infinite grace and power. All that God is, and . . . has, is at the disposal of prayer. Prayer can do anything God can do, and as God can do anything, prayer is omnipotent."[23]

Prayer can move mountains. It can change hearts and transform families. It can impact neighborhoods and even nations. It is powerful.

God spoke through the prophet one day and said, "For I know the plans I have for you, declares the LORD, plans for welfare and not for evil, to give you a future and a hope. Then you will call upon me and come and pray to me, and I will hear you. You will seek me and find me, when you seek me with *all* your heart"[24] (emphasis mine).

The word "all" in "when you seek me with all your heart" is numeric. In other words, God is saying if "all of you" will seek me, you will know the plans I have for you. I love how this pictures a community coming together to seek the Lord. If you want to see God's power and blessings in your children, your family, your place of work, your church, your city, and your world… start praying together.

One morning, about 9 days after Jesus ascended into heaven, the Holy Spirit came and indwelled 120 of His followers. By that very evening, 3,000 devout Jews and Gentiles had joined them. Most of them had come to Jerusalem for Pentecost from other countries. Many of them decided to stay in Jerusalem, to learn more about Jesus and to become a part of the phenomenon we now call the church. And it all started with a prayer meeting.

▶ IN REAL LIFE
FINDING A PRAYER PARTNER

Praying with a community starts one person at a time. Find someone who can be your prayer partner. I promise it will be life-altering and game-changing.

Praying with a prayer partner can be informal, like praying with a pastor after a church service or a friend in your small group. It can also be a more formal relationship with someone you commit to praying with regularly. Do you want to find an ongoing prayer partner, but don't know where to start? Let me help you.

Step 1. Ask God to bring the right person to your mind.
Literally pray, "God would you bring someone to mind that I can pray with?" Ask Him to show you someone who is trustworthy, who is growing in his or her faith, who is willing to be vulnerable, and who is available and willing to pray with you.

Step 2. Invite that person to pray with you.
Don't overthink it. It can be as simple as texting prayer requests to each other, praying over the phone, or meeting in person to pray. You'll have someone to open up to, someone to share blessings with, and someone to pray over. There are a million ways to go at it. The important thing is committing to the process of praying together consistently.

Step 3. Be the prayer partner you are looking for.
Zig Ziglar said, "If you go looking for a friend, you're going to find they're very scarce. If you go out to be a friend, you'll find them everywhere."[25] The same can apply to prayer partners.

Be the prayer partner you need. Find some people and ask them if you can pray for them. Chances are one of these people will ask you the same question in return.

Step 4. Read the Bible together.
We all know the value of sharing a meal with others. Reading the Bible is similar to eating food. You can do it alone, but you are missing something if you never share it with others. Select random books or chapters of the Bible to read together. Sometimes I like to ask friends to read through Proverbs with me in a month. We read one Proverb each day (there are 31 of them) and text each other the verse that means the most each day.

Step 5: Encourage each other.
One of the greatest benefits of having a prayer partner is the encouragement you find. Find ways to build each other up, especially when life tears you down. Paul said to "encourage one another and build one another up."[26]

You were created both to know God and to be part of a community. Praying, reading the Bible, and being an encouragement to others fulfills both of these purposes in your life.

CHAPTER 3
IT MUST BE MORE THAN SUNDAY

Do you remember when you became a new Christian? How excited you were when you realized that you were forgiven and that Jesus was your Lord and Savior? How you felt when you understood that Jesus was preparing a home for you in heaven? There is nothing like it.

The year was 1980. My parents had recently given their lives to Christ. That summer, I attended my very first Vacation Bible School where I trusted Christ as my personal Lord and Savior. Did I understand everything as a 5-year-old? Of course not. But I knew that I was a sinner and that Jesus loved me enough to die for my sins on the cross.

This kid walked out of VBS excited and full of joy. I remember running up to my parents and telling them about the decision I had made. They couldn't keep me quiet! I couldn't wait to get back to church for Sunday School. Even though I was only a child, I knew that I had experienced a change on the inside.

Why do new Christians get so joyful like that? It's because they know that Jesus performed a supernatural work in their life. As a result, they are eager to know more about Him and to be with other Christians.

This is what happened to a small group of people in the book of Acts after their lives were radically transformed by the Gospel of Jesus Christ.

> "And they devoted themselves to the apostles' teaching and the fellowship, to the breaking of bread and the prayers. And awe came upon every soul, and many wonders and signs were being done through the apostles. And all who believed were together and had all things in common. And they were selling their possessions and belongings and distributing the proceeds to all, as any had need. And day by day, attending the temple together and breaking bread in their homes, they received their food with glad and generous hearts, praising God and having favor with all the people. And the Lord added to their number day by day those who were being saved"[1]

Who were "they" at the beginning of this passage? "They" were the apostles and all of the people who had given their lives to Christ.

Pentecost had just happened. The Holy Spirit came. Peter preached a powerful message about Jesus Christ. What happened next was beyond words. The Bible reports, "those who received his word were baptized, and there were added that day about three thousand souls."[2]

How crazy is that! 3,000 people gave their lives to Christ that day. At their second public gathering, over 5,000 were added to the church. And those numbers kept growing and growing. It is estimated that 100,000 people were a part of the church in Jerusalem after 25 years. The population was around 200,000 at the time.

What we have here is a church of 100,000 people in a city of 200,000. Half of the city had come to trust Christ as their

Lord and Savior! It's no wonder the high priest said, "You have filled Jerusalem with your teaching."[3]

Imagine what it would have been like to be a part of the church back then. To experience a house church gathering with all of these early Christians. To partake in communion together. To worship without years of church traditions. It would have been amazing.

One of the things that fascinates me most about the early church was how they did life together. It was so much more than just sitting in rows listening to someone on a platform teach. They made friends in real life. In addition to large gatherings, they met in homes all around the city… and more than just on Sunday.

EITHER/OR OR BOTH/AND?

Today most churches meet on Sunday mornings. For some, it's Sunday mornings and Wednesday nights. And for the super committed (or crazy lol), it's Sunday mornings, Sunday nights, and Wednesday nights. Yep, three times.

How frequently are we supposed to meet? Once, twice, three times a week? On what day? Sunday?

Let me start by mentioning that the word "Sunday" does not appear in any place in the Bible. Sunday has traditionally been regarded as the "first day of the week" or "the Lord's day" in the New Testament. These phrases are found eight times. Three of the eight mention the church gathering on that day, although the third was written by the Apostle John while presumably alone on the Isle of Patmos. They are:

- "On the first day of the week, when we were gathered together to break bread, Paul talked with

them, intending to depart on the next day, and he prolonged his speech until midnight" (Acts 20:7).
- "On the first day of every week, each of you is to put something aside and store it up, as he may prosper, so that there will be no collecting when I come" (1 Corinthians 16:2).
- "I was in the Spirit on the Lord's day" (Revelation 1:10).

I may have missed a verse or two, but the point remains the same. There are only a handful of references to the church meeting on Sunday.

On the other hand, there are several references that directly state (or imply) that the early church didn't just meet once a week, but every single day. They are:

- "And day by day, attending the temple together and breaking bread in their homes, they received their food with glad and generous hearts" (Acts 2:46).
- "And every day, in the temple and from house to house, they did not cease teaching and preaching that the Christ is Jesus" (Acts 5:42).
- "But when some became stubborn and continued in unbelief, speaking evil of the Way before the congregation, He withdrew from them and took the disciples with Him, reasoning daily in the hall of Tyrannus" (Acts 19:9).
- "Praising God and having favor with all the people. And the Lord added to their number day by day those who were being saved." (Acts 2:47).
- "So the churches were strengthened in the faith, and they increased in numbers daily" (Acts 16:5).

- "Now these Jews were more noble than those in Thessalonica; they received the word with all eagerness, examining the Scriptures daily to see if these things were so" (Acts 17:11).
- "But exhort one another every day, as long as it is called "today," that none of you may be hardened by the deceitfulness of sin" (Heb. 3:13).

When you read the New Testament, it's hard to miss that the early church met more than just on Sundays. The idea of doing church once or twice a week under the direction of one pastor or teacher would have been foreign to them.

Gene Getz writes:

> "The Bible certainly does not dictate any patterns in this area [how many meetings and when]. There is little said in the New Testament about when the church met. Some would even question that meeting on Sunday is an absolute guideline for the church, but rather an example of when the church met."[4]

While there are some examples of the early church meeting on Sundays, these are examples – not mandates. In other words, while there are examples of Sunday gatherings, it is not commanded anywhere in the New Testament that the church must meet on Sunday.

Should we throw out Sunday services and go back to daily gatherings? No.

It's not either/or.

It's both/and.

IT'S NOT ABOUT THE PLACE

The early church didn't go to church. They were the church.

They met together not as the end goal, but as a way to equip themselves to be the community God wanted them to be and to do the work God intended them to do.

In the New Testament, they met in public places like schools, rented rooms, and in the outer court of the Temple. Those Temple courts provided a large space where hundreds (maybe thousands) of them could meet together at a time.

> The early church didn't go to church.
> They were the church.

However, they most often met in private homes. Several times you read about "the church in so-and-so's house." Church historians tell us that this was the norm for the first several hundred years of the church. Building "church buildings" as we know them for large gatherings doesn't seem to have been a priority for them. They were flexible. They met and ministered wherever they could.

The earliest building devoted to Christian use is at Dura Europos on the Euphrates River in eastern Roman Syria. It was a house that came into Christian possession and was remodeled in the 240's. Two rooms were combined to accommodate a large group and another room became a baptistery.[5]

The early church didn't argue over when and where they should meet. They knew that church was more than a building. Jesus had freed them to worship anywhere as long as it was in spirit and in truth.[6] This still applies today. He gives the freedom to worship in church buildings, in homes, in school gymnasiums, in offices, in hotel conference rooms, and anywhere else.

Nowhere in the New Testament do we read, "The church needs to meet in houses because it's a family." The Bible also doesn't say, "The church needs to build auditoriums large enough to seat everyone."

I will say that meeting in smaller groups, house to house, seems to have some advantages.

Rick Warren shares four of these advantages:

> It is infinitely expandable.
> It is unlimited geographically.
> It is good stewardship.
> It promotes relationships.[7]

Today, most churches meet in a dedicated church building. Many of those who don't have a permanent building are longing for the day they can find or afford one. Having a church building large enough for everyone makes sense, although I do think we should consider how the layout of our churches have the potential to inhibit community. Are we effectively growing in community when we sit in rows like spectators, staring at the backs of each others' heads?

We will talk about the effectiveness of rows later in this chapter. But my point right now is that worship is not about the space where you meet. It is about the spirit in which you meet.

Donald Norbie said:

> "What did the early church do? There are no rules about buildings in Scripture. The early church was flexible and adaptable, determined to survive in every environment."[8]

I am not advocating for selling your church building and ditching your scheduled church services. The pendulum can swing two ways. On one extreme, you can have a weekend spectator event at a church building with little or no community happening. On the other extreme, you have people meeting in homes because they see the home as the only place real community can be formed. Which is it?

It's not either/or.

It's both/and.

WHAT'S THE BLUEPRINT FOR BUILDING COMMUNITY?

Finding an authentic community has always taken work. I am convinced that it takes even more work in the virtual world that we find ourselves in. We are so advanced in so many areas, yet so behind when it comes to meaningful relationships. You can have hundreds of friends online and at the same time be lonely.

This is one of the reasons why the U.K. recently appointed a Minister of Loneliness to tackle what the Prime Minister called a "sad reality of modern life" for many people.[9] How do we combat loneliness? What's the blueprint for building real community in a virtual world?

Let's look at the first church — the church at Jerusalem. Those early Christians didn't know anything about building community. They had no precedent. There were no gurus to consult with. They had no church leadership podcasts or books to read. They didn't even have the New Testament. Yet, it was done Jesus' way and they were able to build a strong community that impacted the world.

So how do you build community in your life? What's the blueprint? I don't have it all figured out, but here are some things I am learning from the early Christian community in the book of Acts.

1. TALK BIBLE WITH YOUR FRIENDS.

> "And they devoted themselves to *the apostles'* teaching and the fellowship, to the breaking of bread and the prayers."[10] (emphasis mine)

The early church was devoted to teaching. The word "devoted" is sometimes translated, "committed." They were committed to the Word of God.

Beginning with Moses and with all the prophets, the apostles explained to the people the things concerning Jesus in all the Scriptures.[11] At their meetings, the apostles – those who had lived with Jesus and witnessed His death and resurrection – would teach. How awesome would that be?

Can you imagine if Peter showed up to talk with you today? To hear his stories, to ask him questions, and to eat a meal with this one who knew Jesus personally? Wow, that would be amazing! While the apostles can't be with you to teach in person, you still have their teaching. It's the New Testament.

An understanding of what God says in His Word is the basis for your walk with God. You can't live out what you don't understand. You can't claim promises that you've never heard. You can't stand on verses that you don't know.

There's a battle taking place in your mind. The enemy comes against you every day with thoughts of insecurity, doubt, fear, and worry. His goal is to keep your mind so filled with lies that it overtakes you. You have to take "every thought captive"[12] by remembering what God has told you in His Word.

The Bible talks about a man named Job. He lost everything. It didn't look like things would ever turn around when he was told, "God will fill your mouth with laughter and your lips with shouts of joy."[13] This was in chapter 8 of Job. Things didn't turn around until chapter 42. I can imagine Job sitting there discouraged, feeling sorry for himself, thinking that things would never turn around. But then he remembered what God promised. He remembered that God would fill his mouth with laughter.

You may be going through loss and disappointment, but your story isn't over yet. Get in the Bible and read the promises that God speaks over your life. I believe He is going to fill your mouth with laughter once again.

> You may be going through loss and disappointment, but your story isn't over yet.

Like Job, remember what God says. When you spend time in His Word, it will change your perspective.

Study the Bible when you are by yourself and in the company of others. There is something special about sitting together with friends and learning from God's Word together. It's an important rhythm to incorporate into your life.

Some of my best friends are people that I "talk Bible" with. We text each other verses. We share links to sermons or podcasts that have challenged us. We benefit from each other's insights and perspectives. We ask questions like "What has God been teaching you lately?" and "What do you think the Bible says about this?"

Deuteronomy 6:7 encourages you to talk about God's Word when you get up, when you lay down, when you are at home, and when you are on the way. This includes when you are with your friends.

Sometimes I refer to the Bible as a love letter from God. While it seems like love letters are mostly a thing of the past, the idea is still the same. I remember some of those love letters I received from Beth back in the day. I treasured them and read them slowly and carefully several times. I even smelled them. (Yes, I'm weird like that.) The Bible is God's love letter to you. Read it as often as possible both by yourself and with others.

2. SPEND TIME WITH LIFTERS.

"And they devoted themselves to the apostles' teaching and *the fellowship*, to the breaking of bread and the prayers.[14]" (emphasis mine)

Having friends in real life requires a commitment to spending time together. The Greek word used for "fellowship" is *koinonia*. It expresses the idea of having something in common with somebody else.

A community is an organized group of people that share something in common. It can be a love of classic Ford Broncos (that's me), branding and marketing (that's Beth), or anything else like politics or food or sports. There's something special about meeting up with other people who share the same interest. As Christians, we share something in common – Jesus. He is our common ground. He holds us together.

Acts 2 goes on to elaborate about what *koinonia* looked like. It included communal-style living, where they "had everything in common." They sold property to give to anyone in need. They gathered regularly in large groups, as well as in homes. They shared meals, and more.

You don't need to live in a communal home in order to live out *koinonia*, but authentic fellowship is far more than saying hello over a donut at the church or leaving a comment on someone's social media post. It requires time. It's hard to love people that you never spend time with.

Take a look at the people you are spending time with. Proverbs says if you walk with wise men, you will become wise. It says not to spend time with a hot-tempered person, or you'll become hot-tempered. It also says to not hang around with people that talk too much, or you will talk too much yourself.

There are two kinds of people – Lifters and Downers. Some people are Lifters. They lift you up. They inspire you and help you to go farther. Other people are Downers. They push you down with their negativity and "can't do" mindset.

This is hugely important because our spirits rub off on each other. If you spend time with excellent people, excellence will rub off on you. If you hang out with generous people, you'll become more generous yourself. If you associate with motivated people that dream big, those qualities will rub off on you as well.

This is why it's so important that you are selective with the people you choose to spend time with. Spend time with dream builders, not dream dashers.

> Spend time with dream builders, not dream dashers.

A few years ago when our family was in Fort Myers Florida, we visited the vacation home of Thomas Edison. I was fascinated to learn that Edison, Harvey Firestone, and Henry Ford each had vacation homes next door to each other. They were friends and would spend much of the winters together. They didn't spend time with just anyone. They hung around other big thinkers, visionaries, and achievers. No wonder they did such amazing things.

Proverbs 27 says, "Iron sharpens iron, and one man sharpens another."[15] Spend time with people who are sharpening you and making you better.

3. REMEMBER THE CROSS.

"And they devoted themselves to the apostles' teaching and the fellowship, to *the breaking* of bread and the prayers."[16] (emphasis mine)

I have always assumed that "the breaking of bread" referred to observing Communion, or the Lord's Table. When you study the New Testament, it can refer to both observing Communion or simply eating meals together. The early church did both and sometimes it is hard to know which it is referring to. Either way, they regularly came around the table to both remember Jesus and also engage in building community.

I'll speak more about eating meals together in a few pages. For now, let me address Communion.

One day, Jesus "took a cup, and when he had given thanks He said, 'Take this, and divide it among yourselves….' And He took bread, and when He had given thanks, He broke it and gave it to them, saying, 'This is My body, which is given for you. Do this in remembrance of Me.'"[17]

Jesus wanted them to observe Communion "in remembrance of Me." Communion is supposed to invoke memories. You remember how lost you were without Jesus. You remember how arrogant and into yourself that you were. You remember how spiritually blind you were. But then you remember "at the cross, at the cross, where I first saw the light, and the burden of my heart rolled away".

Communion reminds you of the greatest truth in the world – that Jesus loved you and gave Himself for you so that you could be forgiven and reconciled to God! When you partake of Communion, you remember the power of what Jesus did when He died for you.

It not only helps you remember His sacrifice on the cross, but it is also a powerful way to bring us closer together. Jesus said, "Do this in remembrance of Me." The opposite of the word remember is dismember. Dismember means to be pulled apart.

Because we are human, it's easy to allow disagreements and offenses to pull us apart from each other. Husbands and wives that were once united are at odds. Friends that once stuck together through thick and thin no longer speak to each other.

When you come to Communion and remember the great sacrifice that Jesus made on the cross, how can you not forgive someone? How can you hold on to that grudge? When we come to Communion we remember… and relationships that are dismembered can be restored!

There is one additional thing I want you to point out about the very first Communion. Jesus told His disciples, "Enter the city. Go up to a certain man and say, 'The Teacher says, My time is near. I and my disciples plan to celebrate the Passover meal at your house.'"[18] Jesus planned on using the upper room of a house to serve Communion before He died on the cross.

Jesus initiated Communion in a house. Jesus made it a house experience, not just a church experience. You don't have to wait for church on Sunday to remember the Lord's death and resurrection. Find some crackers and grape juice, bread and water, or whatever you have that pictures the body and blood of Jesus. Eat and drink and remember His great sacrifice for you on the cross. There is nowhere in the Bible that says you have to partake in Communion at church or you have to use certain elements. It's your obedience to Him that matters the most.

> Jesus initiated Communion in a house. Jesus made it a house experience, not just a church experience.

4. STAND IN THE GAP.

> "And they devoted themselves to the apostles' teaching and the fellowship, to the breaking of bread and *the prayers*."[19] (emphasis mine)

It's good to pray for yourself. You can pray for wisdom, favor, strength, courage, and so on. While it's important to pray for those things, don't stop there. There are people that God has put into your life that need you to pray for them.

The Bible tells us to, "Pray one for another."[20] In Acts, the early church gathered together to pray. I want you to follow their example and take time to pray for others.

Look around at the people in your family, those whom you work with, and your neighbors down the road. I bet you know a co-worker that is struggling or someone in your church that has cancer. When God brings those needs to your mind it's not an accident. Pause and pray for them.

Pray for others… and pray with others.

These first Christians prayed together a lot! 48 times in the book of Acts it says, "they prayed." They remembered Jesus' promise: "If you ask me anything in my name, I will do it."[21]

One of the greatest decisions you can make in your quest to find friends in real life is to join others in prayer. You've probably heard the saying, "Families that pray together stay together." The same is true with friends.

In the Lord's Prayer, have you ever noticed that the pronouns are plural and not singular?

> "Our Father in heaven, hallowed be your name. Your kingdom come, your will be done, on earth as it is in heaven. Give us this day our daily bread, and forgive us our debts, as we also have forgiven our debtors. And lead us not into temptation, but deliver us from evil."[22]

In the Lord's Prayer, we are reminded that while we can pray individually, there is power in praying with others. We all know the importance and the power of prayer; yet if we are honest, it is an area of weakness for so many of us. We often struggle in prayer because we go at it all alone.

You need others to help you win in life. Rarely does a single player win a game entirely on his or her own. A single soldier seldom declares victory in his or her own strength. There are battles you can't fight alone. They must be won in prayer.

> ▶ There are battles you can't fight alone.
> They must be won in prayer.

God said in Ezekiel, "I looked for someone among them who would build up the wall and stand before me in the gap on behalf of the land so I would not have to destroy it, but I found no one." Back in those days, cities had huge walls around them to protect them from the enemy. But at times, things would happen to the walls that would create a gap. When there was a gap, the enemy could come in. When this happened, they would place one of their best armed soldiers to stand in that gap until the wall was repaired.

People all around you have broken-down walls. They are fighting loneliness and depression. They don't think they will ever get out of the hole they are in. There's a breach in their wall. God is asking you, "Will you stand in the gap?" Be a warrior that stands in the gap for people around you. Pray for them and with them.

5. LOVE THROUGH YOUR GENEROSITY.

> "And all who believed were together and had all things in common. And they were selling their possessions and belongings and distributing the proceeds to all, as any had need."[23]

The early church was famous for their generosity. They literally shared everything—with one another and anyone with a need.

I am not suggesting communal living for you and your family. The situation in Jerusalem was somewhat unique. Thousands of pilgrims had traveled there for Pentecost. Many had come to faith in Jesus after Peter's message and they wanted to stay longer to get grounded in their new faith. They needed hospitality and financial help to do this. To meet these needs, the church opened their homes and their wallets to help those who needed it. Some even sold land and donated the proceeds.[24] They demonstrated a commitment to generosity.

I love the story of Jesus inviting himself to Zacchaeus' house for lunch. Zacchaeus was a tax collector, notorious for getting rich at the expense of his neighbors. Everyone hated him, but Jesus moved toward him. I love that about Jesus. He always moves toward the abhorred and outcast.

Do you have a heart for those that need your love the most? When you start loving the unlovable, criticism will follow. This happened with Jesus. The people criticized Him for sharing a meal with Zacchaeus.

After listening to Jesus, Zacchaeus declared that he would repay anyone he had cheated (plus interest) and that he would give half his wealth to the poor. Jesus replied, "Today salvation has come to this house."[25] Jesus wanted everyone to know that Zacchaeus had changed! Isn't it interesting that the evidence of Zacchaeus' salvation was generosity.

How generous are you with the people around you? From a young age, we're told that it's better to give than to receive. This sounds like a cliche, but it turns out that there's a lot of truth to those words. According to psychologist John Gottman, kindness and generosity are the two most important qualities for successful relationships.[26]

Rick Warren says:

> "One of the best ways to learn to love is through generosity—giving your time, money, effort, and energy. When you're generous, you're affirming that God and people matter most to you. In other words, what matters most is love.
>
> Every time you give—whether that's giving your time, your money, your effort, or your energy—you reveal what matters to you. Tell me how you spend your money and your time, and I'll tell you what matters most to you.
>
> If at the end of your life you've acquired a giant pile of things but you're estranged from your family and friends, you've missed the point! You've missed the opportunity to love through your generosity."[27]

Paul told the church in Corinth, "see that you excel in the grace of giving."[28] He could have said, "I want you to excel in education, in sports, or in business." Those are all good. But he said, "I want you to excel in giving."

Look for little ways to be a big blessing to others. Beth was at the airport a few weeks ago and saw an airport employee emptying the trash can. The terminal was hot, crowded, and full of grouchy people. Beth walked up to him and gave him a $20 bill followed up with "I want you to know I see you working hard. Thanks for everything you do." His face lit up. You would have thought he just won the lottery.

> Look for little ways to be a big blessing to others.

I heard a story about a young man that grew up very poor in a small city. He would go door to door selling different items to try to pay his way through college. At one point, he only had a dime to his name. He was so hungry that he hadn't eaten a decent meal in a couple of days. He got his nerve up and decided that at the next house he knocked on, he was going to ask them for something to eat.

A very attractive young lady answered the door. She was about 16 years old. When he saw how beautiful she was, he lost his nerve and wouldn't ask for anything. She said, "You look like you're starving. Can I get you something to eat"? He said, "No, I'd just like a drink of water."

She went in and brought him back a big glass of cold milk. He thought he had died and went to heaven. He hadn't had milk in the longest time and couldn't ever remember being able to drink a whole glass. He drank it down all in one big gulp. He went to reach into his pocket for the dime to pay the young lady. She said, "No, you don't owe me anything. My mother taught me to never accept money for an act of kindness."

Years later, that young lady became seriously ill. She was treated in the local hospital in the small town, but doctors couldn't find out what was wrong with her. They sent her away to the big city to the leading specialist, a man named Dr. Howard Kelly. When Dr. Kelly saw on her chart the city she was from, he was very intrigued. He rushed down to her room, took one look at her, and immediately recognized her.

Dr. Kelly took on this case personally. He went to great lengths to do everything he could to make sure she got well. Sure enough, 4 months later she had totally recovered and was ready to leave the hospital. Dr. Kelly requested that his business office send the bill through him personally so he could approve. The woman dreaded looking at the bill, knowing that it would probably take her a lifetime to pay it off. But when she opened that bill, Dr. Kelley had written in big letters, "Paid in full with one glass of cold milk."

Never forget that when you're generous to people in their time of need, God will make sure somebody will be kind to you in your time of need.

6. GO DEEPER WITH OTHERS.

"And *day by day*, attending the temple together and breaking bread in their homes, they received their food with glad and generous hearts"[29] (italics mine)

The early church was devoted to meeting together. They didn't just gather on Sundays, but every day through the week. They spent time in each other's homes, breaking bread and sharing life.

It takes more than just seeing someone once a week to make real friends and build an authentic community. It's hard to be close to someone that you only see once a week at church.

While it's important to gather with the whole church for worship and teaching, we benefit most relationally from those we get to know on a personal level. If you only attend the Sunday morning service at your church, but never spend time getting to know the people in the church outside of those scheduled service times; you won't fully enjoy the *koinonia* that God wants for you.

> It's hard to be close to someone that you only see once a week at church.

A few years back I was listening to the Catalyst Podcast. Andy Stanley was talking about what would happen to North Point Church if something happened to him. Here's what he said:

> "Let's say that something happens to me, all the staff, and all the buildings simultaneously explode. Let's make it the worst case scenario. There's no staff. There's no buildings. And there's no me. Here's what would happen. On Monday, Tuesday and Thursday of the following week, thousands and thousands of adults would gather in homes all over the city and pray together, and do Bible study together and take care of whatever family members are left over and the church is going to go on. Because at the end of the day, circles are better than rows. And from day one, we've been committed to creating a culture that's all about circles and not rows. We are famous for our rows. But the strength of our churches is what happens in circles."

Acts says that every day the early church was "attending the temple together and breaking bread in their homes."[30] I love this. They would get together to pray, worship, and be taught followed by some food. I probably like this part so much because I love eating! Beth and I are true foodies. Are you? This is a bit of a rabbit trail, but here's how you can tell.

If you're a foodie:

- You don't eat fast-food (or you don't enjoy eating fast food).
- You'll try any and all foods.
- You think about your next meal before anyone else.
- The restaurants you eat at on vacation are just as important as the place you stay at.
- A party is only good if there is good food.
- You rank the holidays by which ones have the best food.

Whether you are a foodie like us or not, food has a great way of connecting people. When you study the life of Jesus, you find that He spent a lot of time eating with people. Something special happens when you eat with others. Sharing a meal or a cup of coffee really deepens relationships.

> When you study the life of Jesus, you find that He spent a lot of time eating with people.

It's interesting that their meals were so often referred to as "breaking bread." I like to think this suggests that these weren't elaborate feasts, but just simple meals. I see breaking bread as simple as throwing a frozen pizza in the oven or making some grilled cheese. If you wait to eat with people until your house is just right and the menu is perfect, you'll never do it. Just invite some people over and share a simple meal.

Commit to moving beyond Sundays and building relationships during the rest of the week as well. Invite someone to share a cup of coffee or to meet you for lunch. Maybe you could have ice cream on Saturday night with a family you haven't seen much lately. If God lays someone on your heart, pick up the phone and give them a call. Start breaking bread and building community.

7. BE GOOD TO PEOPLE.

> "And day by day, attending the temple together and breaking bread in their homes, they received their food *with glad and generous hearts*" (italics mine)

Jesus was constantly blessing the people around Him. The Bible says, "Jesus went about doing good, healing all that were sick".[31] The first thing Jesus did before helping people was just to be good to people.

One day as an act of care and concern, Jesus humbled Himself and washed the feet of His disciples. Then He said, "You also ought to wash one another's feet."[32] He went on to add a new commandment: "Just as I have loved you, you also are to love one another."[33]

Jesus was always good to people. What would happen if you followed His example and found someone to bless every day? The number of your real friends would skyrocket.

Everywhere you go, look for opportunities to be good to people. It doesn't have to be big things. Bring your co-worker a cup of coffee in the morning. Buy someone their fountain drink at the gas station. When you are in front of a long line of people, hold the door open and smile.

Sometimes all it takes is asking the Holy Spirit to lead you to someone who needs it the most. Is there a cancer-filled person that you can drive to their chemo treatment? Are there parents learning to care for a child with special needs that could use a night out? Is there a new family in your community that would love an invite over for ice cream?

Beth and I want to be known for being good to people. We talk about this a lot. If we take you out to eat, we will buy your meal. If we are around your children, we are going to be good to them. If you ask for help, we are going to say yes. We don't want to be known for our ministry or one of our businesses. When people talk about Ryan and Beth Frank, we want them to say, "They are so good to people!"

There is no greater feeling than in making somebody else's day. Choose to bless someone every day. Paul said, "as we have opportunity, let us do good to everyone."[34] The more you bless others, the more God will bless you and the more attractive you will be to those around you.

THE MOST IMPORTANT THINGS AREN'T THINGS

Our girls love campfires. I like them too, I just don't like starting them. Fire starting is a challenge for me. But once I get lucky enough to actually start it, I enjoy it. Imagine a campfire. When the logs are together, they burn hot and bright. Pull one log out and what happens? Before long the flame dies and the embers cool until it's finally cold and dead. I've seen this happen to too many people. Don't let it happen to you.

I read a poem recently called "Heaven's Surprise." It goes like this:

IT MUST BE MORE THAN SUNDAY

I was shocked, confused, bewildered
as I entered Heaven's door,
Not by the beauty of it all,
by the lights or its decor.

But it was the folks in Heaven
who made me sputter and gasp
the thieves, the liars, the sinners,
the alcoholics, the trash.

There stood the kid from seventh grade
who swiped my lunch money twice.
Next to him was my old neighbor
who never said anything nice.

Herb, who I always thought
was rotting away in hell,
was sitting pretty on cloud nine,
looking incredibly well.

I nudged Jesus, "What's the deal?
I would love to hear Your take.
How'd all these sinners get up here?
God must've made a mistake.

And why's everyone so quiet,
so somber? Give me a clue."
"Hush, child," said He. "They're all in shock.
No one thought they'd see you."

    We are going to be spending a lot of time together in heaven. Let's start doing real life together now!
    My prayer is, "God, help us to love each other and not to be so busy we forget that the most important things in life

aren't always things. I pray that we wouldn't just go to church but we would be the church." Paul describes the church as people dedicated to doing whatever it takes to reach out and help each other.[35]

Jennie Allen sums it up well when she said:

> "Living in deep community with other people will be hard, messy and scary – we can promise you that. But we can also promise that your life will be filled with so much joy that you won't be able to imagine living any other way."[36]

Devote yourself to life together. It must be more than Sunday.

▶ IN REAL LIFE
QUESTIONS TO ASK SOMEONE OTHER THAN "WHAT DO YOU DO?"

We've all been in the awkward situation of meeting someone new and not knowing what to say. If you're like many people, you break the awkward silence with a question like "How are you?" or "What do you do?" Here are some questions to help you really get to know someone better.

What's the most interesting thing that's happened to you lately? One thing that everyone has in common since Adam and Eve is that we like to talk about ourselves. This question allows them to share a personal story and you can share one back.

If you could travel anywhere in the world, where would you go? You'll learn a lot about their family, hobbies, and interests with this question.

Do you have a small or big family? This gives you a chance to not only learn about their family, but to share about yours.

What do you do for fun? How someone spends their free time will tell you a lot about them. You might find you have something in common.

What is your favorite food or meal? Again, Beth and I are foodies so we like asking this question. We normally discover a new place to eat or food to try.

What is your favorite memory as a kid? These stories are always fun and normally involve some smiles and laughter.

What is something you are looking forward to? This is more of a forward-looking question than backward-looking. The answers are all over the map.

What is something big you are working on right now? I love asking people this question. It tells me how they think based on their definition of "something big."

What's the last picture you took on your phone? This question is totally random and normally opens the door to a great conversation about work or family.

Regardless of which questions you choose, the important thing is to ask open-ended questions that will create conversations. What questions do you like to ask other than "What do you do?" Let's learn from each other. Text me and let me know. (765) 441-4598

CHAPTER 4
THE POWER OF TEAMWORK

As a kid in school, I always disliked team projects. Let's be real... I hated them. I liked the kids. I liked the work. I just didn't like when the teacher split us into groups for projects that were going to result in a grade. It seems like 9 times out of 10, my grade would get held hostage by someone else's failure to do their part. I would end up being the kid (or one of a few kids) spending extra time doing someone else's work for them. Maybe you had a similar experience.

How do you feel about team projects? More than likely they either energize you or they frustrate you. Do you think, "This group motivates me and the team effort is producing something creative and innovative," or do you think, "These people are slowing me down. Get me out of here."?

Whether you enjoy teamwork or you shy away from it, God doesn't want you to work alone.

Your life was never created to be a solo endeavor. God created you for community. John Wesley said, "The Gospel of Christ knows of no religion but social; no holiness but social holiness."[1] God has designed us to live in relationships.

Paul painted quite a picture when he said, "For as in one body we have many members, and the members do not all have the same function, so we, though many, are one body in Christ, and individually members one of another."[2]

To help you understand what Paul was teaching, think of the Christian community as your local Walmart. (Minus the people walking around in their pajamas at 3:00 in the afternoon.) You have one big store with many different departments. One department can do things another department cannot, but they all have the same goal. In a similar sense, the church has many parts but we are all the same body. We are all part of the same team.

God doesn't want you to be a lone ranger. Yes, God loves you as an individual and calls you as an individual to follow Him. However, well-intentioned efforts to emphasize the importance of a personal relationship with God can inadvertently diminish the importance of your relationship with others. It doesn't end with just "Jesus and me."

God has saved us individually to become a community:

> "You are a chosen race, a royal priesthood, a holy nation, a people for His own possession, that you may proclaim the excellencies of Him who called you out of darkness into His marvelous light. Once you were not a people, but now you are God's people; once you had not received mercy, but now you have received mercy."[3]

When we come to faith in Christ, we obtain citizenship in God's kingdom. We aren't lone rangers; we are indelibly linked to God's people. If we imagine that life is just about "Jesus and me," we won't function as a team.[4]

Teamwork is all around us in life. We see it in schools, sports, businesses, and on reality TV. We are quick to retweet or share motivational quotes like, "Teamwork makes the dream work!" while dismissing it in our own lives – and to our own detriment.

Success in life and ministry hinges on your willingness to go at it as a team.

FINGERPRINTS OF FAVOR

Beth and I are grateful for the people He has placed in our lives. We have been able to partner with so many good people over the years – most of which have been much smarter than us! We look back at the success stories of our lives and see both the fingerprints of God's favor and the value of the team around us.

I'll never forget the Sunday of 2006 that God impressed it on our hearts to publish a magazine for children's ministry leaders. On the drive home from church that spring Sunday evening, I somewhat apprehensively told Beth that I sensed God telling me that we should launch a magazine. We had discussed the need for a publication like this for the children's ministry community, but it never entered either of our minds that we would be the ones to actually do it. Much to my surprise, Beth proceeded to tell me that the Lord had put that very same thing on her heart earlier that same day. That was a serious God moment for us both!

We immediately found ourselves excited… and scared! We were children's pastors ourselves at a small church in Indiana, we were barely out of our 20's, and I should also mention that we were broke.

We had no clue how we would pay for this thing. We knew nothing about editing and design. We didn't know where to go to print a magazine. We didn't know how to sell ads. And we for sure didn't know how we would get children's pastors around the world to subscribe. But we also knew that when God gives a vision, He always gives the provision.

As we both prayed about this, God kept bringing Jeremiah 33:3 to our minds. "Call to Me, and I will answer you, and show you great and mighty things, which you do not know." We began to beg God for great and mighty things that were bigger than what we knew. That word "mighty" in the Hebrew can also be translated "hidden" and means "that which is inaccessible."

We needed God to give us what seemed to be inaccessible. We needed wisdom that wasn't our own. We needed money that we didn't have. We needed a team that wasn't there. We needed connections that seemed unfeasible.

One by one, we began to ask people to join our team. And one by one, they said yes. We started reaching out to curriculum publishers asking them to buy ads. In that first issue of the magazine, it was "name your price" advertising. We would take anything.

Within three months of that spring Sunday drive home from church, we were holding a magazine in our hands. An editorial team had been assembled. A printer had been found. Advertisements had been sold. We even had enough money to pay the printer bill when it arrived in the mail.

Eighteen years later, we still print *KidzMatter Magazine*. It was called *K! Magazine* back then. Some of you might remember that. We have a great team and thousands of children's pastors benefit from each issue that we print. To God be the glory, great things He has done! It would have never been possible without God's favor and an amazing team around us.

It doesn't stop there.

God's provision gave us confidence for what else He was capable of.

When we decided to launch The KidzMatter Conference, a national conference that attracts thousands of children's ministry leaders each year, we knew it was way bigger than just us. It would require a team. We started asking and people started responding.

One day a colleague recommended that Beth and I read Robert Kiyosaki's book, *Rich Dad, Poor Dad*. We read it and we knew that we wanted to begin investing in multi-family housing. We wanted to create assets. This was a big dream and we knew it would take the right people to make it happen. After a breakfast meeting (with who would become our real estate partner and one of my best friends, Caleb Crandall) and investing time into relationships, the dream came to life.

We knew absolutely nothing about operating a car wash and a drive-thru convenience store, but we knew we wanted to do something for our daughter with special needs. Beth had some great ideas for branding, marketing, and gourmet soda recipes; but we knew that if Luci's Car wash and Drive-Thru was going to succeed, we needed a power team.

Then there was the day we decided that leading a 501(c)3 organization, running a national conference, partnering in a real estate firm, and operating a car wash with a drive-thru convenience store that is open 6 days a week wasn't enough. We needed one more project added to the mix. (Cough. Cough.)

Beth and I gave each other another good look and agreed that we must be crazy, but YOLO so let's trust those crazy ideas. We decided to launch Frank Insurance Management. We knew that to build an agency that is more customizable, more responsive, and higher-tech; we would need the right people on our team.

Here is the biggest lesson we have learned: Much of our success in life is a result of God's favor and the power of a team.

> ▶ Much of our success in life is a result of God's favor and the power of a team.

Steve Jobs said it, and I couldn't agree more, "Great things in business are never done by one person."

There is power in teamwork.

GREAT THINGS BEGIN IN PRAYER

The Apostle Paul experienced a radical transformation after meeting Jesus Christ on the road to Damascus. In the chapters to come, we will learn from his commitment to the community and his passion to see God's people working together as a team.

Paul went on three missionary journeys to carry and spread the Gospel of Jesus Christ across the ancient world. How did these missionary journeys of his begin? We find ourselves in a church prayer meeting.

> "Now there were in the church at Antioch prophets and teachers, Barnabas, Simeon who was called Niger, Lucius of Cyrene, Manaen a lifelong friend of Herod the tetrarch, and Saul. While they were worshiping the Lord and fasting, the Holy Spirit said, 'Set apart for me Barnabas and Saul for the work to which I have called them.' Then after fasting and praying they laid their hands on them and sent them off."[5]

Here we meet the church of Antioch and some of the members of this community. "Barnabas, Simeon who was called Niger, Lucius of Cyrene, Manaen a lifelong friend of Herod the tetrarch, and Saul."

A few of these names will mean little or nothing to you. A few you may recognize. But they are each a great reminder that the church is made up of simple ordinary people. Just look around your church and the church down the street and the church further down the next street. Then take a look at the church all around the world. It's made up of everyday people like you and me.

The word translated "church" is from the Greek word *ekklesia*, which means "the called out." If you have trusted Christ as your personal Savior, you – ordinary you – are "the called out" and are part of the church. And this is all by God's design!

Let's look at a few of the people that were a part of the church community at Antioch. You know the name Saul (later known as Paul). We have been talking about him in this book.

You probably know Barnabas. Barnabas was a Levitite from Cyprus whose given name was Joseph. He was so encouraging that he was given the nickname Barnabas, which means "son of encouragement." I can't wait to meet Barnabas in heaven one day. Like Barnabas, I want to be an encourager. We'll talk more about the power of encouragement later in Chapter Five.

But who is Simeon, or Lucius, or Manaen?

Simon was nicknamed "Niger," a Latin word meaning "black" or "black skinned." Simeon is believed to be from Africa and is sometimes thought to be Simeon of Cyrene who carried the cross of Jesus.

Lucius is a Greek name. He was from Cyrene, a city in North Africa.

Manaen was a very interesting person. He is described as a lifelong friend of Herod. This is the same Herod that had John the Baptist beheaded. Some of the other translations say, "brought up with." The Greek word translated "life-long friend" or "brought up with" is a compound word which means "nursed with". Manaen may have been a foster brother of Herod's or a very close friend.

What a diverse group at this church! This is a beautiful picture of an unlikely group of everyday people coming together to shoulder kingdom work and live together in community.

I fell in love with the book of Revelation back in my seminary days. One of my professors went through the book verse by verse and it blessed me beyond measure, just as the book of Revelation promises it would. "Blessed is the one who reads aloud the words of this prophecy, and blessed are those who hear, and who keep what is written in it, for the time is near."[6]

In the book of Revelation, John gets an all-access backstage pass to see what happens in heaven. He tells us about a gathering of a great multitude of people that were too many to count. They all wear white robes. They all hold palm branches in their hands. They all shout one phrase. They are unified. But they aren't all the same.

John doesn't see the similarities in these people, but rather the differences. He observes that every nation, tribe, people, and language is represented. Here is what we learn: Heaven is diverse. It's beautiful. It's perfect. It's what God wants. It's also a picture of what God wants our communities to look like as well. And when they do, we get a little bit of heaven right here on earth.

▶ Heaven is diverse. It's beautiful. It's perfect.

FRIENDS IN REAL LIFE STAND TOGETHER

This unlikely group of everyday people in Antioch had gathered with the purpose of worship and fasting when the Holy Spirit spoke to them and said, "Set apart for me Barnabas and Saul for the work to which I have called them."

I'm amazed at how worship and fasting will open my ears to the voice of the Holy Spirit in my life. Have you experienced this?

We don't talk about fasting much, but it's an important spiritual discipline that we should each be practicing. Have you ever fasted while seeking wisdom and power from God for an important decision? When you fast, you are saying, "God I need spiritual food more than I need physical food. My focus is on you, not on my stomach."

In addition to fasting, the church prayed for Barnabas and Saul. Prayer moves the hand of God.

John Knox was a Scottish minister, Reformed theologian, and writer who was a leader of the country's Reformation. He was considered one of the most powerful preachers of his day, but interestingly only two of the hundreds of sermons he preached were ever published. He is a key figure in the formation of modern Scotland, yet there is only one monument erected to him in Scotland, and his grave lies beneath a parking lot.[7]

Billy Graham once said:

> "John Knox prayed, and the results caused Queen Mary to say that she feared the prayers of John Knox more than she feared all the armies of Scotland. John Wesley prayed, and revival came to England, sparing that nation the horrors of the French Revolution. Jonathan Edwards prayed, and revival spread throughout the American colonies. History has been changed time after time because of prayer. I tell you, history could be changed again if people went to their knees in believing prayer. Even when times are bleak and the world scorns God, He still works through the prayers of His people. Pray today for revival in your nation, and around the world."[8]

Prayer is powerful. Never forget the power of a praying community. Your time spent in His presence is never wasted or regretted. It is the place where the Holy Spirit aligns your heart to His and you hear His voice speak.

> Your time spent in His presence is never wasted or regretted.

After fasting, praying and hearing the voice of the Holy Spirit, the church laid their hands on Paul and Barnabas and commissioned them to do God's work. We continue this practice when we ordain pastors, missionaries, and many others for all kinds of Kingdom tasks. We also do this when we pray over people.

Laying on of hands is a symbolic gesture that communicates, "We are in this together. We support you." It is a physical act of standing together with someone.

It's not just Barnabas and Saul that were a team, but they were part of the larger church community. The laying on of hands reminded them that they would always be part of the team in Antioch.

THE FUEL THAT BRINGS UNCOMMON RESULTS

Barnabas and Saul had already been serving together. They had developed quite a track record by this time. We read about them several times previously in the book of Acts.

Barnabas and Saul were what I call a power team. They were friends. They worked well together. Their gifts even complimented each other. Barnabas was the encourager while Paul was the bold preacher.

The calling God has placed on your life is best fulfilled through teamwork. Nowhere in the Bible do we find independence encouraged by God. You were created for community!

> Nowhere in the Bible do we find independence encouraged by God. You were created for community!

Andrew Carnagie said, "Teamwork is the ability to work together toward a common mission. It is the fuel that allows common people to obtain uncommon results."

A big reason Paul's first missionary journey was so effective was because it happened in the context of a team. Teams are vital to success.

We see this all throughout the Bible:

- God gave Moses the vision to build the tabernacle, but he did not do it himself. God gave him a man named Bezalel, who had "skill, intelligence, knowledge, and all craftsmanship" (Exodus 35:31).
- Solomon understood the wisdom of working as a team. "Two are better than one, because they have a good reward for their toil" (Ecclesiastes 9:4-12).
- God gave Ezra the dream to rebuild Israel after the Babylonian captivity. However, he did not do it alone. He gathered leaders from Israel to go with him. "I took courage, for the hand of the LORD my God was on me, and I gathered leading men from Israel to go up with me" (Ezra 7:28).
- The prophet Elijah took Elisha with him when he felt depressed and like he was burning out. (1 Kings 19)

- Jesus surrounded Himself with a team in order to change the world. Very few of His disciples seemed to be world-changing leaders. He called a group of uneducated, unknown people willing to do something significant together.
- Jesus even sent 72 out in ministry teams. (Luke 10:1-24)

Paul and Barnabas worked as a team. They first sailed to the island of Cyprus, which was Barnabas' home territory. They arrived at Salamis and taught in the synagogues along with John Mark, Barnabas' cousin. The three continued preaching across the whole island and finally arrived at Paphos on the opposite side. In Paphos, the proconsul, Sergius Paulus, summoned Paul and Barnabas because he wanted to hear the Word of God. However, a Jewish false prophet and magician, Elymas, tried to prevent the proconsul from coming to faith. Paul, filled with the Holy Spirit, struck Elymas blind and performed his first miracle. When seeing this miracle, the proconsul believed. Paul and Barnabas then set sail from Paphos to go into modern-day Turkey while John Mark set sail to return to Jerusalem.

In Turkey, Paul and Barnabas made their way to Antioch (the one in Turkey, not the one in Syria where they came from). There, they taught in the synagogue and many put their faith in Christ. However, the following week when nearly the entire city gathered to hear their preaching; some Jews began contradicting them and stirred up trouble for Paul and Barnabas. After this rejection of the Gospel from the Jews, Paul said that they were turning to the Gentiles. "When the Gentiles heard this, they began rejoicing and glorifying the word of the Lord, and as many as were appointed to eternal life believed."[9]

Eventually being driven out of Antioch by the Jews, Paul and Barnabas went to Iconium and taught in the synagogue there. Many believed, and Paul and Barnabas performed signs and wonders during their stay in Iconium. Over time, however, the city became divided between those who followed the Jews and those who sided with Paul and Barnabas. When they learned that the opposition was planning to stone them, they fled to Lystra, Derbe, and the surrounding area.

In Lystra, Paul performed another miracle – healing a man who had been crippled since birth. Unfortunately, the miracle caused the people to believe that Barnabas was the god Zeus and that Paul was Hermes, the messenger and chief spokesman of the gods. Paul and Barnabas had to work hard to convince the people that they were mere men and prevent them from making sacrifices to them. Then Jews from Antioch in Turkey and from Iconium came and persuaded the crowds to stone Paul. After the stoning, Paul was dragged out of the city and left for dead. However, when the disciples gathered around him, he got up and walked right back into Lystra. The next day, he and Barnabas went to Derbe and shared the Gospel where many more put their faith in Jesus Christ.

Upon completing their time teaching in Derbe, Paul and Barnabas retraced their steps returning through Lystra, to Iconium, and to Antioch in Turkey to encourage the believers there and appoint elders in each church before making the trip home to Antioch in Syria. To get from Antioch in Turkey to Antioch in Syria, they passed through Perga and set sail from Attalia, taking the time to share the Gospel in both places.

The entire missionary journey is believed to have taken twelve to eighteen months. In Antioch in Syria, Paul and Barnabas "gathered the church together, they declared all that God had done with them, and how He had opened a door of faith to the Gentiles."[10]

10 BENEFITS OF TEAMWORK

Are you secretly a lone-wolf-meets-control-freak, believing that nobody can ever do a job as well as you? Have you been burned in the past by someone who was supposed to be a team player? Don't let those keep you from working with others. The benefits are too great.

Henry Ford said, "Coming together is a beginning. Keeping together is progress. Working together is success." You were created for community. Together, everyone truly does achieve more.

Solomon said it this way:

> "Two are better than one, because they have a good reward for their toil. For if they fall, one will lift up his fellow. But woe to him who is alone when he falls and has not another to lift him up! Again, if two lie together, they keep warm, but how can one keep warm alone? And though a man might prevail against one who is alone, two will withstand him—a threefold cord is not quickly broken."[11]

Solomon knew the power of teamwork. He lists four benefits and then I'll add several more.

1. TEAMWORK BRINGS COURAGE.

Solomon said, "Two are better than one, because they have a good reward for their toil." On a good team, two can accomplish more than each one individually. The sum is always greater than the parts.

In 1519, the Spanish explorer Hernan Cortez wanted to capture the treasure that the Aztecs were holding. He landed 11 ships on the Yucatan shore with 500 soldiers and over 100 sailors. Despite the large contingent of soldiers, he was still greatly outnumbered by the large Aztec empire on shore.

Some of the men in Cortez's army questioned his leadership feeling that his nearly impossible mission would only end in failure. These ringleaders plotted to seize some of the vessels to escape to nearby Cuba.

When Cortez learned of these plans, he made it impossible for the conspirators to get away, making sure everyone was devoted to one united plan. Cortez gave the command to burn his own ships.

Naturally, the men at first resisted this seemingly insane directive as they knew they weren't going to be able to return home. Cortez's response was, "Well then, if we want to return home we are going to have to take their ships!"

His plan was simple - with their own ships taken out of the picture, any possibility of failure was also removed. They would have to have 100% dedication to the cause so they could succeed and take their enemy's ships to return home. And they did exactly that.

They found the courage that sometimes only comes on a team.

2. TEAMWORK PROVIDES PROTECTION.

Secondly, Solomon says that a friend will help in times of trouble. "For if they fall, one will lift up his fellow. But woe to him who is alone when he falls and has not another to lift him up!"

In an accident, it sure helps to have someone else around. This is a problem that many retired people who live alone face.

My grandmother recently fell and was unable to get to the telephone. It took nearly eight hours before someone was there to help her. For others, it can be a day or two before a neighbor checks in on them. So it's better that two be together.

Sometimes you fall down physically and need help getting up, but the principle has an even greater emotional and spiritual application. When you stumble in your spiritual walk or are weighted down with heavy emotions; it's critical to have a friend who can come alongside you in your walk with God.

Paul told the Galatians:

> "Dear brothers and sisters, if another believer is overcome by some sin, you who are godly should gently and humbly help that person back onto the right path. And be careful not to fall into the same temptation yourself. Share each other's burdens, and in this way obey the law of Christ."[12]

3. TEAMWORK BRINGS COMFORT.

You have to have grown up in the cold mid-west to fully appreciate the third benefit. When the temperature is below zero outside, you understand what Solomon means when he says, "If two lie together, they keep warm, but how can one keep warm alone?"

The winter nights in Palestine, where Solomon was writing this, are comparatively cold. Especially for the poorer inhabitants, the outer garments worn by day were used as the only blanket at bedtime.

Friends sure have a way of warming the heart. Are you there to offer comfort to a friend in need? Do you offer words of love and encouragement? Be the friend that makes someone laugh a little harder, cry a little less, and smile a lot more.

4. TEAMWORK MEANS THAT SOMEONE HAS YOUR BACK.

If two is company and three is a crowd, sometimes it is good to have a crowd... especially if someone is coming against you.

We have a serious problem with crimes on our streets today. Often it is the person who is alone who is the victim of crime. Though one may be overpowered, two can defend themselves. There is strength in numbers. Solomon reminds us that a cord of three strands is not quickly broken.

Paul told the church at Philippi:

> "If you've gotten anything at all out of following Christ, if His love has made any difference in your life, if being in a community of the Spirit means anything to you, if you have a heart, if you care—then do me a favor: Agree with each other, love each other, be deep-spirited friends. Don't push your way to the front; don't sweet-talk your way to the top. Put yourself aside, and help others get ahead. Don't be obsessed with getting your own advantage. Forget yourselves long enough to lend a helping hand.
>
> Think of yourselves the way Christ Jesus thought of Himself. He had equal status with God but didn't think so much of Himself that He had to cling to the advantages of that status no matter what. Not at all. When the time came, He set aside the privileges of

deity and took on the status of a slave, became human! Having become human, He stayed human. It was an incredibly humbling process. He didn't claim special privileges. Instead, He lived a selfless, obedient life and then died a selfless, obedient death—and the worst kind of death at that—a crucifixion."[13]

You need a community that has your back. You also need to have the back of the people around you.

In addition to what Solomon had to say, here are some other benefits of working as a team.

5. TEAMWORK IMPROVES CULTURE.

How is the culture at your place of work? Culture answers the question, "How do we do things around here?"

Encouraging teamwork and collaboration is part of a healthy culture. Rather than encouraging competition, a culture of teamwork creates opportunities for people to work together and use all available resources and skills to reach the goals of the organization. When people see themselves as part of a team, they understand that thinking, planning, decisions, and actions are better when done cooperatively.

> ▶ When people see themselves as part of a team, they understand that thinking, planning, decisions, and actions are better when done cooperatively.

The writer of Hebrews encouraged us to, "consider how to stir up one another to love and good works."[14] The phrase "stir up" is from the Greek word *paroxusmos*, from which we get our English word, paroxysm, which literally means, "a sudden violent emotion or action."[15] This can have a negative implication (a paroxysm of rage) or a positive implication (a paroxysm of laughter).

I want to be the kind of person that is always stirring others to love and to good works. When people come in contact with me, I want them to be stirred up to love and good works. Beth and I want to create this culture in the organizations that we lead. And we want the same for you.

6. TEAMWORK MAKES THE WORK FUN.

As I mentioned at the beginning of this chapter, I always hated team projects as a kid. I'm a little older now and I've learned that they aren't that bad after all. Sure, you're going to have a far-from-ideal team member now and then. And yes, it can be rewarding to get a project of your own accomplished, but it's a lot more fun to work with other people.

When you work with others, you find the support and encouragement you need along the way. You can be there for each other when things are tough and celebrate together when things go as planned.

A Gallup study of nearly 7,500 full-time employees found that 23 percent of employees feel burned out at work very often or always. Another 44 percent say they sometimes feel this way. What helps? Sharing the load at work.

"Team members can provide emotional support to each other because they often understand the demands and stress of completing work even better than managers," says Ben Wigert, lead researcher for Gallup's workplace management practice.[16]

7. TEAMWORK BRINGS INCREASED POTENTIAL FOR INNOVATION.

According to Frans Johansson, author of *The Medici Effect*, some of the most innovative ideas happen at "the intersection" – the place where ideas from different industries and cultures collide.

"Most people think success comes from surrounding yourself with others that are like you," says Johansson. "But true success and breakthrough innovation involves discomfort. Discomfort pushes you to grow. This is where differences of experience, opinion, and perspective come in. Diversity is a well-documented pathway to unlocking new opportunities, overcoming new challenges, and gaining new insights."

A recent report from the consulting firm McKinsey & Company backs this up. It found that teams made up of members from diverse backgrounds (gender, age, ethnicity, etc.) are more creative and perform better by up to 35 percent, compared to more homogeneous teams. Instead of looking at an issue from your individual vantage point, you get a 360-degree picture, which can lead to an exponential increase in ideas.[17]

Grow your network and grow your results. Hang with the same old crowd and you'll get the same old results.

8. TEAMWORK IMPROVES PRODUCTIVITY.

Michael Jordan said it best when he said, "Talent wins games, but teamwork and intelligence win championships." That is so true.

Working as a team inspires people to work harder. It's crazy but true! Scientists have found that team members actually motivate each other to be more productive. In a team, work is shared among people with different skill sets and expertise. Members join together to do a better job and in a shorter time frame than one single person ever could.

The TINYpulse Employee Engagement and Organizational Culture Report surveyed more than 200,000 employees. Participants reported that having the respect of their peers was the #1 reason they go the extra mile at work.[18]

Start working as a team and I promise productivity will go up.

9. TEAMWORK LEADS TO BETTER PROBLEM SOLVING.

When it comes to solving problems, are two (or more) heads really better than one? Yes, they are.

Albert Einstein gets all the credit for discovering the theory of relativity, but the truth is that he relied on conversations with friends and colleagues to refine his concept.

Science reinforces the idea that many brains are better than one. "We found that groups of size three, four, and five outperformed the best individuals," says Dr. Patrick Laughlin a researcher at the University of Illinois at Urbana-Champaign. "[We] attribute this performance to the ability of people to work together to generate and adopt correct responses, reject erroneous responses, and effectively process information."[19]

If you have a problem to solve, consider how bringing others in and working as a team might influence the outcome. The advantage of working with others often comes from the shared ideas and being able to draw upon the experience and expertise of multiple people.

10. TEAMWORK KEEPS YOU SHARP.

There may be no "I" in team, but being part of a team is good for you. You will meet new people. You will be forced to consider new ideas. You'll find the courage to try new things. You will even learn from the mistakes of the people around you.

> There may be no "I" in team, but being part of a team is good for you.

You've heard the saying, "If you're not growing you're dying." There's a lot of truth to this. In Stephen Covey's book, *The 7 Habits of Highly Effective People*, the seventh habit is about the need to continually develop and taking time to "sharpen the saw."

Proverbs says, "You use steel to sharpen steel, and one friend sharpens another."[20] You need people in your life that will keep you sharp.

Gary Ott is one such person to me. I drive past his office on my way to KidzMatter HQ. We serve on the Board of Trustees together at Indiana Wesleyan University. Gary owns and operates over 20 nursing homes in Indiana and Florida. He loves the Lord, his family, and business. About every 6 months I will call Gary to ask for help working through management problems at work or helping me navigate challenges I am facing with my team. Friends like Gary keep me sharp.

To be effective, you must sharpen the saw. You must commit to renewing yourself physically, spiritually, mentally, and socially. This often happens best in the context of a team – not in isolation.

WHAT TEAM ARE YOU ON?

Are you ready to start working as a team like never before? Teamwork is well worth the effort. It's not accidental… It's highly intentional. Your success in life and ministry depends greatly on being a team player.

Paul's first missionary journey was fascinating… from his first miracle to his stoning, and from his bold messages and courageous encouragement for new believers; the entire journey reads like a well written adventure book. The lessons learned from this first missionary journey are many and we barely scratched the surface in these pages. Lessons about worship, suffering, working in teams, dividing and multiplying, and partnering with churches are all included in this first journey.

I want to end this chapter by asking you to consider what teams you are a part of. Do you view yourself as part of a team in your home, at your place of work, or at your church? You are an important team member!

The mission of Jesus is accomplished through teamwork. You have an important contribution to make as a team member. Your gifts, abilities and perspective are needed on the team.

Teams are powerful.

▶ The mission of Jesus is accomplished through teamwork.

▶ IN REAL LIFE
7 FORCES THAT SABOTAGE TEAMWORK

In my experience working with both ministry and marketplace teams, I have discovered there are 7 forces that will sabotage teamwork.

1. Confusion
When there is a lack of clarity, a team will begin to make their own rules. Maybe they hear mixed messages, changing messages, or the message is the same but is being communicated poorly. The remedy to confusion is clarity.

2. Know-It-Alls
Teamwork comes from having a "we" not "me" mindset. Yet, know-it-alls find their way on a team. Ego is a natural repellent of collaboration. Ball hogs always kill teamwork. Learn to value the shared knowledge and input of others.

3. Insecurity
You will never rise above your level of insecurity. Insecure people don't want to work with a team because they don't want to look smaller than everyone else or they are driven by fear. Insecurity kills teamwork.

4. Shutting down ideas
Saying "no" more than "yes" will sabotage team work. Give others on your team permission to dream, innovate, create, and trust their crazy ideas.

5. Not spending enough time together
Relationships take time and energy to grow the way they need to. You may be busy, but find the time to invest in your team.

Finding the time means putting it on your calendar just as you would a meeting.

6. Distrust

Teams move at the speed of trust. Stephen Covey says, "When trust goes down — in a relationship, on a team, in a company, in an industry, with a customer — speed decreases with it."[21] Trust is built when what we say and what we do match. A lack of trust will kill teamwork immediately. Division is game over.

7. Avoiding conflict

Where there's movement, there will be friction, and friction is uncomfortable. Good judgment and appropriate action to intervene during times of friction and conflict are marks of great team players.

CHAPTER 5
SO GLAD YOU'RE HERE

As a child, I loved going to visit my Grandma Cleta. She lived in a white farmhouse that sat at the end of a curved driveway with beautiful weeping willows and a creek along the driveway. I have so many special memories on the farm.

She didn't care if we made a mess upstairs. We could pound on the piano to our heart's content. We could pull some great (and dangerous) stunts on the stairway banister. We could run in and out of the house as much as we wanted. She always fed us three square meals a day. (By the way, her homemade noodles were to die for!) There were always cookies in the jar or a pie in the refrigerator. She loved us with her actions and not only by saying "I love you." She loved spoiling her grandkids rotten and loved making us feel welcome.

During the week, grandma's friends would come over to play cards or dominoes. Ladies from her Sunday School class would come over to make noodles for the church. Holidays were her favorite because all of the family would come to her house for a feast like none other.

My grandma earned the title of Mrs. Hospitality. She loved it. But being hospitable is not something only for grandmas. It's for all of us.

These days people prefer to hit a drive thru or call in a pizza. The thought of preparing a meal or having someone over to the house seems like a giant chore. We don't have time to sit and play games with friends. We're way too busy.

Somehow, we have forgotten what it means to practice hospitality.

SHOWING LOVE TO OTHERS

The Oxford definition of hospitality is: "The friendly and generous reception and entertainment of guests, visitors, or strangers."

The word hospitality in the Bible is taken from two Greek words to make one word. They are the words *philo* meaning love and *xenia* meaning strangers. Biblical hospitality is literally a love for strangers as seen in Hebrews when it says to "show hospitality to strangers."[1]

Hospitality is more than cooking food and entertaining people. It is about loving people. God doesn't want us to only love our family and friends, but even strangers and those different from us.

You are "God's workmanship, created in Christ Jesus for good works."[2] A practical result of having your life transformed by Jesus is that you love everyone, including strangers. This is the true essence of hospitality. Jesus said, "When you give a banquet, invite the poor, the crippled, the lame, the blind, and you will be blessed."[3]

> A practical result of having your life transformed by Jesus is that you love everyone, including strangers.

Although hospitality is of utmost importance in the Bible, it is becoming less and less normal.

Fred Liggin said:

> "In American Christianity, hospitality has not only lost its moral dimensions, it no longer plays an integral role in informing a church's missiology or ecclesiology. Hospitality has been reduced to cozy dinners with friends or associates who closely resemble the socio-economic status and socio-political worldviews of their hosts. Perhaps more detrimental, hospitality has been relegated as one of many Christian practices from which Christians can choose, a practice most generally situated around various forms of table fellowship."[4]

That was such a good quote that I hope you'll read it again. Especially this part: "Hospitality has been reduced to cozy dinners with friends or associates who closely resemble the socio-economic status and socio-political worldviews of their hosts. Perhaps more detrimental, hospitality has been relegated as one of many Christian practices from which Christians can choose..."

Hospitality doesn't only seem to be fading away in the church, but in our culture at large.

People are becoming more and more reliant on themselves. We all grew up hearing the phrase, "The only person you can depend on is yourself." We were taught in elementary school that it's not good to lean on others too much and we need to learn to be independent. Then we go to high school and college and are taught that success goes hand in hand with self-dependence. Anything, we were told, can be achieved through hard work — which usually implies doing it oneself.

The truth is that self-dependence is a double-edged sword. While you need to be able to stand on your own two feet, self-dependence can rob you of the community you were created for. You have to find the balance between dependence on yourself and healthy interdependence with others.

MEET A DYNAMIC DUO

History is full of dynamic duos. We all know them: Mark Antony and Cleopatra, Romeo and Juliet, Mike and Carol Brady from the Brady Bunch, and last but not least - Ryan and Beth Frank. (I see your eyes rolling... and rightfully so!)

The Bible also records some dynamic duos. Abraham and Sarah, Hosea and Gomer, Esther and King Ahasuerus, and Ruth and Boaz are just a few.

One of my favorite married couples in the Bible was Priscilla and Aquila. We first meet them in Acts 18. Before I tell you their story, let me share a few fascinating facts about them.

First, I love their names. Besides the fact that it's fun to say their names together (say Priscilla and Aquila three times softly, it's kind of fun), the meaning of their names is significant. The name Aquila means "'eagle" and the name Priscilla means "little Prisca." Prisca was her formal name and Priscilla was more like a nickname. My wife, Elisabeth, is rarely called by that name. People who know her best call her Beth (or if you are her grandmother you call her Bethie). That the writers felt comfortable using Priscilla's nickname makes me think she was a down-to-earth person who made friends with everyone.

Secondly, when we meet them for the first time, we learn that they were tent makers. I take the mention of their vocation to indicate that ministry was not their full time job. There is important work to do for those in full-time vocational ministry, as well as those who work full-time in the marketplace. I have heard Beth say it a million times, "All of life is sacred." People who are in full-time vocational ministry play an important role in furthering God's kingdom. But those who aren't in formal ministry make an equal, if not greater, impact in moving God's kingdom forward.

Thirdly, I love that whenever they are mentioned in the Bible, they are always mentioned together. They were such a dynamic duo that their names are always side by side. What's even more interesting is the order in which their names are mentioned. In the seven references to this couple, the wife (Priscilla) is mentioned before the husband (Aquila) five times. This is uncharacteristic in the Bible and suggests that Priscilla played a leading role in their ministry. Go girls!

OPENING A ROOM, A SEAT, AND SOME DOORS

Priscilla and Aquila had come to the Greek city of Corinth from Italy as victims of Roman persecution. Around the year A.D. 49, the Emperor Claudius issued an edict exiling all the Jewish people from Rome, the seat of the Roman Empire.

Priscilla and Aquila packed their belongings, said goodbye to their friends in Rome, and started fresh in Corinth. They opened a small shop in the city market to work their trade of tent making. The Bible doesn't record whether they had any friends or business contacts who helped them establish their business in a new location. Either way, their decision to start over in a new city required courage and determination.

Working as a team in their small shop, Priscilla and Aquila found they could accomplish more together than they could alone. I get this. Beth and I have always had the privilege of working alongside each other and we love it. It's been a privilege and blessing.

> Priscilla and Aquila found they could accomplish more together than they could alone.

It wasn't long before they met another tent maker — someone who would change their lives forever.

Paul was tired, homeless, alone, and needed a place to stay. In his own words, he came to Corinth "in weakness, fear, and trembling."[5] They cleared out a room. Not for one night, not for one week, but until Paul was called to move on.

Priscilla and Aquila invited their new friend to work with them at their shop. Having no home of his own in Corinth, Paul was sheltered and provided for by this hospitable couple in his time of need as they all worked together as tent makers.

Paul stayed in Corinth for a year and a half teaching the Word of God primarily to the Greeks in the area. Though he did not stay with Priscilla and Aquila the entire time, they must have grown to be very close friends because when Paul set sail for Syria, Priscilla and Aquila went with him. They decided to leave their home and tent making business behind to join Paul as he traveled to do more ministry.

It was a big move.

It reminds me of a story I read recently.

This guy was moving from one house to another just a few blocks away. As he watched the moving crew carelessly grabbing his cherished antiques and tossing them around, he decided that he would move his grandfather clock himself. It was the antique he prized most and he didn't want it damaged.

Taking the clock in his arms, he started for the new house. The clock was as tall as he was and was very heavy, so he had to put it down every few feet to rest his arms and catch his breath. A kid watching from down the sidewalk ran over to him and said, "Mister, can I ask you something?"

"Sure, what do you want?" he asked between catching breaths.

The kid went on to ask, "Why don't you just carry a watch?"

That's about as good as my jokes get. Just ask my girls at home.

Now back to the story.

After landing in Syria, the three made their way west to the city of Ephesus (on the west coast of modern day Turkey). At that time, Ephesus was an important port city for trading merchandise and was home to a large tourist attraction – a temple for the goddess Artemis.

One day, an up-and-coming young evangelist named Apollos, from Egypt breezed into town. After a well-polished sermon, Priscilla and Aquila invited him over for dinner. He was gifted, passionate and accurate in his teaching… but he was off in his theology. Recognizing the opportunity to invest in this young leader, Priscilla and Aquila invited him to their home and spent time teaching him.

At some point during this time frame, Priscilla and Aquila began hosting church services in their home at Ephesus. Week after week, they served the early church. They were committed to growing spiritually themselves, in addition to helping others grow in their walk with Christ.

There are two more places where Priscilla and Aquila are mentioned in the Bible.

One is in Paul's letter to the Romans where we find that their lives have come full circle. They were living back in Rome again after the emperor Claudius had died and the exile had ended. Paul wrote, "Greet Prisca and Aquila, my fellow workers in Christ Jesus, who risked their necks for my life, to whom not only I give thanks but all the churches of the Gentiles give thanks as well."[6]

Paul owed a lot to this couple. They even risked their necks for him! I am looking forward to meeting them in

Heaven one day and hearing their life story first-hand. I am also curious to know how they risked their lives for Paul.

Paul's final reference to them is in his last letter. He was sitting in a Roman prison and writing to Timothy one last time. Timothy was pastoring the church at Ephesus, and Prisca and Aquila were there with him, still shouldering the weekly work of ministry.

To the very end, they were offering hospitality to the community, sharing the Gospel, and serving the Lord.

Prisca and Aquila set an example for us of what hospitality looks like. They simply opened up a room for Paul, a seat at the table for Apollos, and the doors of their home as a meeting place for the church. Their home became a source of encouragement and teaching.

> Their home became a source of encouragement and teaching.

HOSPITALITY AS A SACRED OBLIGATION

Unless you have personally experienced the hospitality of Mid-Eastern culture, there is really no way to describe it. Hospitality is a bedrock of cultures and countries across the Middle East. When Beth and I visited the Holy Land, we experienced it first-hand. It seems ironic to think of hospitality in a part of the world where there is so much conflict and violence taking place. Yet, hospitality in this region is seen as a sacred obligation.

If you go back to the days of the Bible, showing hospitality had a very practical application. For starters, traveling was often dangerous. People on the road were vulnerable to weather, thieves, or even wild animal attacks. Knowing they could count on a safe place to stop made leaving home a little more doable. Living conditions were also harsh and food hard to come by. Because of this, sitting down at a meal and sharing your food and drink with others was seen as the ultimate act of caring and giving.

Job said, "the sojourner has not lodged in the street; I have opened my doors to the traveler."[7] To open your tent and to eat at the table with people not of your own family was considered true hospitality.

One day, Abraham left the shade of his tent to welcome three strangers. As soon as he saw them, he ran out to meet them and then bowed before them. In the Middle East, grown men in their robes don't run. It is considered shameful and humiliating to pull up your robe (exposing your legs) to run.

Abraham humbled himself before these three men and washed their feet. He called them "Lord" and called himself "your servant".

He invited them into his tent to eat with his family. He asked his wife to knead three seahs of flour into bread and to cook it for these three strangers. I don't want you to overlook this part of the story. How much was three seahs of flour? This was 50 to 65 pounds of flour – enough bread for a month! He spared no expense to demonstrate hospitality.

Abraham then ran out into his herd, got a young calf and had it killed, and prepared it to eat. He also had curds (like cheese) brought in to be eaten. While the three strangers ate, Abraham stood by and watched, waiting to serve them.

Only later did he realize he had been entertaining the Lord that day! It turns out that these three strangers were two angels and God himself. You can read about it in Genesis 18. Referring to this story, the writer to the Hebrews said, "Do not neglect to show hospitality to strangers, for thereby some have entertained angels unawares."[8]

It wasn't just Abraham that practiced hospitality. All of Israel was taught "treat the stranger who sojourns with you as the native among you, and you shall love him as yourself, for you were strangers in the land of Egypt: I am the LORD your God."[9]

Isaiah, the prophet of the Lord crying out against the empty forms of fasting, said, "This is the kind of fast day I'm after: to break the chains of injustice, get rid of exploitation in the workplace, free the oppressed, cancel debts. What I'm interested in seeing you do is: sharing your food with the hungry, inviting the homeless poor into your homes, putting clothes on the shivering ill-clad, being available to your own families."[10]

THE ULTIMATE EXAMPLE OF HOSPITALITY

Jesus is the ultimate example of hospitality. When He was making preparation for the observance of Passover and the institution of the Lord's Supper, He arranged for a guest room to house His disciples. He washed their feet and wiped them with a towel.

He placed a cup and bread before them that pictured His sacrifice for their sins. He took the bread saying, "This is my body, which is given for you." Taking the cup, He added, "This cup that is poured out for you is the new covenant in my blood."[11]

He prepared them for when He would no longer be with them. "Let not your hearts be troubled. Believe in God; believe also in me. In my Father's house are many rooms. If it were not so, would I have told you that I go to prepare a place for you? And if I go and prepare a place for you, I will come again and will take you to myself, that where I am you may be also."[12]

He encouraged them to "Abide in me, and I in you."[13] He then poured out His soul in prayer for them.

Jesus was the ultimate host, giving Himself entirely to them. He taught that hospitality is not just a nice gesture, but a necessity. It is not something above and beyond the call of duty, but a command to obey.

▶ Hospitality is not just a nice gesture, but a necessity.

We see this illustrated in the parable of the Good Samaritan. This story was Jesus' answer to the lawyer's question, "Who is my neighbor?" It was the Samaritan who had compassion, bandaged the wounds, poured on oil and wine, carried him on his own animal, and brought him to an inn and took care of the expenses. Then turning to the lawyer, Jesus commanded: "You go, and do likewise."[14]

On the Mount of Olives, Jesus taught that hospitality is a mark of a true follower of His. On the final judgment day, Jesus will say:

> "The King will say... 'Come, you who are blessed by my Father, inherit the kingdom prepared for you from the foundation of the world. For I was hungry and you gave Me food, I was thirsty and you gave Me drink, I was a stranger and you welcomed Me, I was naked and you clothed Me, I was sick and you visited Me, I was in prison and you came to Me.' Then the righteous will answer Him, saying, 'Lord, when did we see You hungry and feed You, or thirsty and give You drink? And when did we see You a stranger and welcome You, or naked and clothe You? And when did we see You sick or in prison and visit You?' And the King will answer them, 'Truly, I say

to you, as you did it to one of the least of these My brothers, you did it to Me.'"[15]

A test of our love for Jesus is our love for others. This is the essence of hospitality. What a rewarding thought that when we give ourselves in hospitality to each other, we give ourselves to Jesus. That is such a privilege and joy.

MAKING FRIENDS IN REAL LIFE

The idea of welcoming friends and strangers into your life comes easier for some than for others. Author Kathy Chapman Sharp says, "Some folks have a natural talent for making guests feel special. Some Christians possess hospitality as a spiritual gift."[16] Maybe like Prisca and Aquila, you are a hospitality-extraordinaire. For you, practicing hospitality comes as natural as riding a bike.

But what about everyone else? I am empathetic to those of you who are introverted, who battle insecurity, or who have been hurt by people you welcomed into your life in the past. God can give you the strength and the courage you need to practice hospitality. Here are some ideas to get you thinking.

1. START SIMPLE.

Sometimes we overthink hospitality. It doesn't have to be that difficult. Don't start by inviting your entire church over for pizza. It might be a good idea to have a block party and invite your neighbors over, but you don't have to start that big.

Choose to spontaneously invite someone over to your home after church. Ask someone to meet you for coffee, send a card of encouragement, call someone and ask about their kids, start a book club, or meet some friends for a bike ride. Start simple.

2. INVITE PEOPLE OVER.

One of the most obvious (and perhaps effective) ways to practice hospitality is to invite people over to your home. However, this can be a challenge for some. After all, your home is your private space. It can get messy and chaotic. It is the one place you can go and be yourself. It is a safe place where you can shield yourself from everyone else. The thought of inviting people over can be uncomfortable and is an act of vulnerability. You are inviting them into a personal part of your life.

Hospitality is not entertaining. It's easy to confuse entertaining with being hospitable, but they are vastly different.

Entertaining involves getting your house Joanna Gaines-worthy. It's laboring hours and hours on FoodNetwork.com trying to find the perfect menu. It requires the playroom to be perfectly clean. It's about having just the right picture on your Frame TV and lighting that Anthropologie candle that you only use on special occasions.

In her flagship book *Entertaining*, Martha Stewart says, "Entertaining, like cooking, is a little selfish, because it really involves pleasing yourself with a guest list that will coalesce into your ideal of harmony, with a menu orchestrated to your home and taste, with decorations subject to your own eye. Given these considerations, it has to be pleasureful."[17]

Hospitality, on the other hand, has nothing to do with candles, or coffee, or ambiance. It has everything to do with putting others first. It focuses on serving, encouraging, and blessing others. The focus is on the conversations you will have and the laughs you will share. Where entertaining often focuses on the host, hospitality focuses on the guests.

> Hospitality, on the other hand, has nothing to do with candles, or coffee, or ambiance. It has everything to do with putting others first.

3. FIND MEAL MOMENTS.

When you study the life of Jesus, you find that many of His striking ministry moments happened around meals. There was the wedding at Cana, a dinner with the despised Zacchaeus, and the Last Supper to name a few. Jesus was even criticized for eating with the tax collectors and sinners.

Find some meal moments. Invite someone to go out to eat. Ask another family to join you for pizza on Friday night. Pay for their meal if possible.

Eating together is one of the most practical ways to overcome barriers between people and build community. It doesn't matter if the meals are high end or simple take-out. What matters is that they involve other people and that they bring you closer together.

4. FIND SOMEONE TO MENTOR.

Look around your workplace or your sphere of influence, and I bet you'll find someone with a few less years of experience. Like Prisca and Aquila, you can make a huge impact in that person's life by being a mentor.

Howard Hendricks was a professor at Dallas Theological Seminary. He would ask his students this question,

"Who are your guys?" He wanted them to always have a small group of people that they were investing time into.

Paul undertook the importance of this. He instructed Timothy, "what you have heard from me in the presence of many witnesses entrust to faithful men, who will be able to teach others also."[18] Show hospitality by investing time in someone else.

5. SIMPLY BE KIND.

Karen Mains says that sometimes practicing hospitality is as simple as being kind. "No business should supersede a smile that conveys, 'So good to have you here.' We can give great healing if we do nothing more than say, 'How glad I am to see you.' Simply by acknowledging others at work, church, and your neighborhood; you're practicing a kind of hospitality that baffles the world."[19]

The true heart of hospitality is captured in this verse, "Whenever we have the opportunity, we should do good to everyone."[20]

It's easy to be kind to people that are being nice to you. But what about that rude person in line behind you? Or that in-law that has a way of pushing your button like no one else? Your natural instinct might be to give it right back to them. Remember, you don't know what put them in that mood. You don't know what they are experiencing at work or at home.

Plato said: "Be kind, for everyone you meet is fighting a hard battle." Do your best to respond to difficult people in a way that would please the Lord. Respond with love. Simply be kind.

6. SHARE YOUR GIFTS.

God has wired you with unique gifts and abilities. What are you really good at? Building things? Encouraging people? Writing? Selling? Maybe you've never met a furnace you couldn't repair. Maybe you love coaching people.

Your gifts or abilities aren't there by accident. God wants you to honor Him with them and to use them to be a blessing to the community around you.

My brother-in-law Jay can fix anything. He knows that whenever I call him it's either because I've broken something or I need to borrow a tool. He has the ability to reverse engineer problems and solve them in a way that I never could. His wife (my sister-in-law) Abby, is a licensed counselor. Beth once had a sign in our house that read, "Who needs a therapist when you have a sister?" Beth has both! Abby is a gifted counselor and is great at listening and giving solid advice and counsel.

How can you use your gifts and abilities to bless those around you? That is practicing hospitality.

7. BE REAL.

It's amazing how attractive you are to others when you are humble and real. Our culture is all about building a false image. It's all about showing our best self – especially on social media. We share our best selves with the world. Whether it's sharing a photo of vacation, or of our kids laughing together on the couch, or the perfect selfie with our spouse; the truth is that we're often only telling half the truth.

The perception is that the smarter, wealthier, and more talented we are; the more people will like and respect us. It's tempting to present an image of ourselves that simply isn't true.

For others, it's not as much trying to build a false image as it is trying to please everyone. People-pleasers want others to like them because it feels good. As a result, they steer their actions in the direction that offers the most approval. On the surface, people-pleasers appear to be selfless, kind, and generous people. However, beneath the surface, they are highly insecure and believe that approval equals value.

Paul addressed this when he asked, "Am I now trying to win the approval of human beings, or of God? Or am I trying to please people? If I were still trying to please people, I would not be a servant of Christ."[21]

Here's the reality. You know you aren't perfect and so do others. You'll never please everyone. Choose to be real, honest, and vulnerable. Choose to admit your total dependence on Christ. Just be real.

8. LOOK FOR SOMEONE YOU CAN BLESS.

We interact with numerous people every day. I wonder how many of these people are outcasts that go unnoticed? Look for the hurting around you.

Martin Luther famously said, "God milks the cow through the milkmaid." God uses people to do the important things in life. In the context of hospitality, He serves people through you!

When you practice hospitality, watch for people who are different from you. Be on the lookout for "strangers." One of the greatest hindrances to building community is that we tend to stratify ourselves.

> One of the greatest hindrances to building community is that we tend to stratify ourselves.

Is the couple sitting by you at church new to the church or to your town? Invite them over for lunch. Do you know a widow that is lonely? Ask her over for coffee. Which of your friends are struggling with their kids at home? Reach out to them.

Paul said to "Share with the Lord's people who are in need. Practice hospitality."[22] Take some time out of your day to stop, look around, and find ways to bless others. Simple acts of kindness can change someone's life forever.

9. WATCH A GAME.

You guys (especially) will like this one. Buy tickets to a sporting event and ask some friends to go with you. Maybe you're like me and you aren't a big sports fan. Do it anyway! A few months ago I bought three tickets to an Indianapolis Pacers game. One ticket was for me, one was for my daughter Londyn, and the other was for Joe in the insurance office. I could not have told you the name of one player to save my life, but that wasn't the point. I wasn't there to watch the game as much as to build relationships and create memories.

If you aren't able to buy tickets to a game, invite some friends over to watch on the TV with you. Sometimes that's better anyway. Call in some pizzas. Have everyone bring some snacks and enjoy each other's company. You'll be amazed at the personal connections that are made.

10. LOOK AT WHAT YOU ARE ALREADY DOING.

Instead of adding things to your calendar, add people. Take a look at what you are already doing that you could invite others into.

Hospitality is more than an event that you organize. It's a way of living. It's about loving and serving people.

Meals are the no brainer on this one. You are already eating, so why not invite someone to eat with you? But it doesn't have to stop with meals. If you are planning a family bike ride, invite another family. If you are opening up the swimming pool for your kids, invite some others to come over for the afternoon as well. There's a lot of freedom to get creative on this one. Just remember, you don't have to add more things to your calendar. Just add people.

BLESSED TO BE A BLESSING

I remember spending two weeks in seminary studying God's covenant to Abraham. The Lord told him:

> "Go from your country and your kindred and your father's house to the land that I will show you. And I will make of you a great nation, and *I will bless you and make your name great, so that you will be a blessing*. I will bless those who bless you, and him who dishonors you I will curse, and in you all the families of the earth shall be blessed"[23] (emphasis mine)

God makes some great promises to Abraham. I want to focus your attention on the promise, "I will bless you.. so that you will be a blessing."[24] God chose to bless Abraham so that he could bless others. The same is true for you. The Bible says, "Give and it will be given to you." If you're not giving away what God has given you, that blessing is not going to continue in the way it could.

Joel Osteen writes:

> "We've all gone through times of difficulty and seen God's goodness. The medical report didn't look good, but God turned it around and now we're healthy. We didn't think we'd ever meet the right person, but God brought us somebody better than we imagined. We lost a loved one and didn't think we could go on, but God gave us strength and peace, and today we're stronger than ever. We were the patient—we needed healing, restoration, favor—and God made a way where we didn't see a way, for which we're so grateful. But it's not enough to just be a grateful former patient. Take it one step further and go from patient to physician.
>
> The apostle Paul said it like this: 'He comforts us in all our troubles so that...when others are troubled, we will be able to give them the same comfort God has given us' (2 Corinthians 1:4). You've been healed; now go help somebody else get healed. You broke that addiction; help somebody else break their addiction. God didn't heal you just so you could be well, but so you could become a healer. He favored you so you could show people favor. He gave you a new beginning so you could help others make it through their loss. You're no longer a patient; you've become a physician."[25]

The purpose of your blessings is to bless others. The result of your blessing others is that you are blessed by God even greater.

> The purpose of your blessings is to bless others. The result of your blessing others is that you are blessed by God even greater.

Choose to bless others with your hospitality. Start simple and start now. Remember, hospitality is more than an event that you organize. It's a way of living. It's about loving and serving people. Paul said to practice hospitality.[26] The more you practice, the easier and more natural it gets. Like Prisca and Aquila, you'll find joy and continued blessings on your life and those around you.

▶ IN REAL LIFE
HOW TO BE HOSPITABLE – EVEN AS AN INTROVERT

If you are an introvert, being with people may not be your forte. More than likely, you appreciate being invited to events and get-togethers, but you're also secretly happy if they get canceled. Introverts, like my wife Beth, need alone time. Being an extrovert, I get energy by being around people. Beth gets energy by being alone. However, introverts can excel at hospitality. Here is how to get started.

1. Start with your friends.
If you start with people you already know, you'll have a great time and won't be nearly as stressed. It will also help with the awkward silence of conversing with someone you don't know and that you are probably dreading.

2. Think small.
You don't have to invite your entire small group over for a pool party. Pick one family and invite them to go out for pizza. If you want to invite someone over to the house, order carry out instead of feeling the pressure to prepare a 4-course meal.

3. Be real.
Focus on getting to know the people you are with, not just entertaining them. Think of some questions in advance that you can ask them. It's all about relationships. People are more comfortable when you express interest in their lives.

4. Lean into your gifts.
Great listening skills come naturally for introverts because they tend to think things through first before voicing their opinions.

Lean into this strength of listening. Choose to listen, ask good questions, and find things you can pray for.

5. Plan time to recover.
Because introverts often feel drained after being with people, it's important to allow time to recover. This might take a few hours or a few days. As introverts, you need time to recharge alone so you're ready soon for more time with people.

Remember, hospitality is not just for the extroverts reading this. It's even for those of you who would prefer to be alone.

CHAPTER 6
SIMPLY ENCOURAGE

Thomas Jefferson and John Adams were the last surviving members of the original American revolutionaries who had stood up to the British Empire and forged a new political system in the former colonies. However, while they both believed in democracy and life, liberty, and the pursuit of happiness; their opinions on how to achieve these ideals diverged over time.

The second and third Presidents of the United States, John Adams and Thomas Jefferson, were good friends in their youth. However, after Adams was replaced by Jefferson, political disagreements separated them and they never saw each other again. The cranky and hot-tempered Adams was a firm believer in a strong centralized government, while the well-read and proper Jefferson believed the federal government should take a more hands-off approach and defer to individual states' rights.

After serving two presidential terms, Jefferson and Adams each expressed to third parties their respect for the other and their desire to renew their friendship. Adams was the first to break the silence. He sent Jefferson a letter dated January 1, 1812, in which he wished Jefferson many Happy New Years to come. Jefferson responded with a note in which he recalled when they were fellow laborers in the same cause.

The former revolutionaries went on to pick up their friendship with over 14 years of correspondence during their golden years.

On July 4, 1826, at the age of 90, Adams lay on his deathbed while the country celebrated Independence Day. His last words were, "Thomas Jefferson still survives." He was mistaken. Jefferson had died five hours earlier surrounded by friends and family. His last words were, "Is it the 4th?" After he heard, "Yes," he breathed his last breath.[1]

The final words of these two Founding Fathers were uttered on the same day, July 4th, as well as on the 50th anniversary of the Declaration of Independence.

A lot of attention is given to a person's final words. Maybe it's expected that they will say something profound, or perhaps offer an apology or a confession of some sort. Just do a Google search of people's final words and you'll find quite an interesting collection.

Some of the most famous last words are credited to Napoleon's sister, Alicia. She observed on her deathbed, "Nothing is as certain as death." And the people around her thought she was dead, until she added, "Except taxes." That's for certain.

Marie Antoinette was the extravagant wife of Louis XVI of France who, according to rumor, dismissed starving peasants with a flippant "let them eat cake." At the height of the French revolution, Louis and Marie were charged with treason and sentenced to the guillotine. While on the scaffold, she accidentally stepped on her executioner's foot and gave him the respectful apology that became her last words. She said, "Pardon me sir. I meant not to do it."

Through time, Christians have made some profound statements near death. Zwingli, a great reformer and contemporary of Luther, said, "They can kill the body but not the soul." William Carey, the great missionary to India, said,

"When I am gone, speak less of Dr. Carey and more of Dr. Carey's Savior." And Susanna Wesley, the mother of John and Charles Wesley, said, "Children, when I am gone, sing a song of praise to God."

Jesus made some profound statements near his death as well. He gathered His disciples together on the day before He was crucified. Judas had gone into the darkness to betray Him. He turned to His other disciples and said, "Love one another as I have loved you."[2] These powerful words were some of His last.

This wasn't simply a suggestion or a thought to consider. It was a command. Jesus knew that we wouldn't always feel like loving, but we could still choose to love - and to love just like He did.

Earlier, Jesus said that when we love as He has loved, we will become a powerful attraction for people who do not know Him. "By this all people will know that you are my disciples, if you have love for one another."[3] Notice He didn't say all people will know that you are my disciples if you go to church... or if you look a certain way... or if you have it all together. Jesus said they'll know by our love for each other.

SIMPLY THE BEST WAY

One of the best methods for loving like Jesus loved is by simply encouraging one another.

Chip Ingram said:

> "Let's face it — life can be really hard. God is good, but in the midst of His goodness, we are still living in the midst of brokenness because we live in a fallen world. God is on our side and He loves us very

much, but that doesn't exempt us from experiencing deep, deep pain. There are times in this life when many of us might find ourselves right on the edge... ready to give up on our marriage, give up on a child or give up on our faith. We might get to the point where we feel like we can't take it any more. When this happens, sometimes the only difference between us going on or giving up, succeeding or failing is a simple word of encouragement."[4]

The world doesn't need any more Negative Nancys and Frustrated Freds. It's a tough world for you and the people around you. As Chip Ingram reminded us, the people around you need a simple word of encouragement.

None of us are immune to the frustrations and discouragement of life.

Dwight Pentecost wrote:

"Discouragement is the loss of courage. When an English word begins with the prefix dis, it simply means that the person being described has lost whatever the rest of the word suggests. The man who is discouraged has lost courage, has lost heart, has lost the will to fight; and the discouraged man is a defeated man."[5]

There are people all around who have lost courage, lost heart and lost the will to fight. They need people like you and me that will choose to be an encouragement.

> There are people all around who have lost courage, lost heart and lost the will to fight.

Simple encouragement is the wind behind our sails. It gives hope. It gives us the strength to carry on. It reminds us of the bigger picture. It keeps us from believing lies. It helps us experience the abundant life that Jesus promised.

The Bible has a lot to say about the importance of a community and how we should encourage each other. As the writer of Hebrews put it, "let us consider how to stir up one another to love and good works, not neglecting to meet together, as is the habit of some, but *encouraging one another*, and all the more as you see the Day drawing near"[6] (emphasis mine). Earlier, the same writer said to "encourage one another daily."[7]

WE ARE STRONGER TOGETHER

Paul and Barnabas were on their first missionary journey. They traveled through modern day Turkey making stops in various cities throughout the region. These two men were a power team.

I define a power team as a group of people with a commitment to one another, to the team, to a high level of living, to a common cause, and to a shared vision. This was Paul and Barnabas.

A power team doesn't compete with each other, they complement each other. (There's a big difference.) Paul was a bold preacher. Barnabas was an encourager. In fact, Barnabas wasn't even his real name. It was Joseph. One day, Joseph was given the nickname "Barnabas," which means "Son of Encouragement," because he was such an encouragement to the people around him.

Their giftings from God complemented each other. Together, they were able to accomplish much more.

Your giftings were not given to you so you could compete with the people around you. Competing will keep you from your destiny.

When you are self-aware and confident in who you are in Christ, you won't view the people around you as competition. You'll see people who complement you and that you can complement in return. Power teams function as a single unit. They are stronger together.

SUCCESS CREATES OPPOSITION

When Paul and Barnabas got to the city of Iconium, they shared about Jesus. They had success presenting the Gospel to both the Jews and the Greeks while there, and ended up staying a long time. But like we often see today, the success created opposition.

Opposition is not a myth. It is real and it comes at you daily. When you begin to rise, expect opposition to follow. You can wish it away, avoid it, and ignore it. The reality is that you must deal with it.

While rebuilding the wall around the city of Jerusalem, Nehemiah faced opposition. Sanballat and Tobiah were rulers in two of the Persian provinces surrounding Judah and were angry that someone had come to help the Jews. They were threatened by Nehemiah's success, but he didn't quit. He kept praying, planning, and working.

It happened to Jesus. The moment He started healing the sick, teaching with authority, and drawing large crowds; the Pharisees began fiercely attacking Him. Occasionally, Jesus would hit back, calling them things like hypocrites and vipers. Other times, He was quiet.

When God begins to bless you with success, prepare yourself. Resistance is coming. You must learn to handle the opposition. The greater the heights you want to reach, the higher the magnitude of opposition that will follow.

Opposition is proof that you are doing something right. Be thankful for the resistance and don't quit. Work even harder.

> Be thankful for the resistance and don't quit. Work even harder.

Opposition followed Paul and Barnabas. God was blessing their ministry and resistance followed. Division came into the city. Some of the people sided with the Jews and some with Paul and Barnabas. It went so far that an attempt was made by some to execute them by stoning them. That is serious opposition!

This forced them to leave Iconium for Lystra (some 20 miles away) and Derbe. This is where their lives started to get really interesting!

As they journeyed, Paul and Barnabas were focused on preaching the Gospel and encouraging the community. Although they didn't travel as miracle workers, they did do some miraculous works. When they arrived at Lystra, there was a man sitting who could not use his feet. He was crippled from birth and had never walked before. He was miraculously healed by Paul which led to Paul and Barnabas being hailed as gods by the people. Paul told them that they were just ordinary men that came to bring the message of Jesus.

Shortly after that, the people who had attempted to stone Paul and Barnabas earlier in Iconium caught up to them. They stirred the people of Lystra up against them. The opposition got so intense that they stoned Paul, dragged him outside the town, and left him for dead.

We can't really understand what it is like to be stoned while trying to preach the Gospel and love people. The experience of being hit with stones on your body and head from many people until they think there is no way you are alive is incomprehensible for us.

ENCOURAGEMENT MEANS BEING THERE

After the stoning, Paul's friends came to be with him. This must have been hours after Paul was stoned and left for dead because if the Jews had seen them, they probably would have stoned them as well.

I want to pause the narrative.

Paul faced opposition. He was stoned. His friends showed up. This is what friends do. They show up.

Biblical encouragement doesn't have all the answers. It doesn't attempt to answer every "Why?" question. It's not limited to giving advice and having the perfect response to every crisis. Encouragement is showing up. It is a shoulder to cry on. It's a listening ear. It's a handwritten note. It's often just by being present. Sometimes the best thing you can do to encourage someone is just be there.

> Sometimes the best thing you can do to encourage someone is just be there.

Just being present can be the best way to encourage sometimes. When you're with someone, you're telling them that they are important and that they matter.

Later, Paul would close his letter to the church at Colosse promising to send his friend Tychicus so that he could encourage their hearts.[8] A person's presence is powerful.

After Paul's friends gathered around him, he came to and got up. It is completely a miracle that he survived this attack. Some think that he had actually been killed and raised to life again, because stoning was usually a reliable form of execution.

When Paul later wrote, "I bear on my body the marks of Jesus"[9], he may have had in mind the scars from this day. He certainly later referred to this stoning when he said, "Three times I was beaten with rods. Once I was stoned."[10]

ENCOURAGEMENT REQUIRES COMMITMENT

What happened next amazes me. When Paul was revived, he didn't run away from the people that stoned him. Instead, he immediately went back to the place where all the danger was. He was committed to the community.

If you get beaten so badly that everyone thinks you are dead, it would take a few days – probably weeks – to recover. Yet, the very next day Paul went to another city to preach the Gospel and encourage the community. What commitment! We see Paul living out his words, "I can do all things through Him who strengthens me."[11]

Why would he do this? I believe he felt a sense of urgency. He was committed to loving like Jesus loved.

Les Parrot writes:

> "If you want to love like Jesus, you've got to …
> become more mindful — less detached;
> become more approachable — less exclusive;
> become more graceful — less judgmental;
> become more bold — less fearful;
> become more self-giving — less self-absorbed."[12]

This was Paul and Barnabas.

Years later, Paul wrote a letter to the Corinthian church. He addressed everything from problems in the church to spiritual gifts. About gifts, he encouraged them to "earnestly desire the most helpful gifts. But now let me show you a way of life that is best of all."[13] He went on to tell them that they were all part of the body of Christ and they should use their gifts to build each other up and glorify Christ. He told them that he was going to show them something even better than any spiritual gift they may have possessed.

Paul said:

> "If I speak in the tongues of men and of angels, but have not love, I am a noisy gong or a clanging cymbal. And if I have prophetic powers, and understand all mysteries and all knowledge, and if I have all faith, so as to remove mountains, but have not love, I am nothing. If I give away all I have, and if I deliver up my body to be burned, but have not love, I gain nothing.
>
> Love is patient and kind; love does not envy or boast; it is not arrogant or rude. It does not insist on its own way; it is not irritable or resentful; it does not rejoice at wrongdoing, but rejoices with the truth. Love bears all things, believes all things, hopes all things, endures all things.
>
> Love never ends. As for prophecies, they will pass away; as for tongues, they will cease; as for knowledge, it will pass away. For we know in part and we prophesy in part, but when the perfect comes, the partial will pass away. When I was a child, I spoke like a child, I thought like a child, I

reasoned like a child. When I became a man, I gave up childish ways. For now we see in a mirror dimly, but then face to face. Now I know in part; then I shall know fully, even as I have been fully known.

So now faith, hope, and love abide, these three; but the greatest of these is love."[14]

Love trumps all. Paul said that we need to have faith, we need to hold on to hope, and we need love as well. He also said that the greatest of the three is love. Fortunately, we don't need to choose between faith, hope, and love. He wasn't trying to make us choose. He wanted us to know that without love, the gifts are meaningless. If you lose love, you lose everything. This is why some of Jesus' final words were "love one another as I have loved you."[15]

I read a story about Franklin Graham and his family. Years ago Jim Baker, the former leader of the PTL Television Network, went to prison for not handling things properly. He admitted he made mistakes and it was a big scandal all over the news. When he was about to be released from prison, Franklin Graham contacted him to let him know that his family wanted to rent him a house and provide him a car to drive. Jim Baker said, "Franklin, you can't do that. I have too much negative baggage. You can't be associated with me, you'll be criticized." Franklin said, "Jim, you were our friend before you went to prison, and you will be our friend afterwards."

The first Sunday he was out, Ruth Graham (Billy Graham's wife) called the halfway house where Jim was staying. She asked the man in charge for permission for Jim to come to church with their family that Sunday. He approved. As he arrived at the church, they took Jim down to the front row and sat him next to Franklin. There were two empty seats next to him and Jim didn't know who they were for. Right before the service started, a side door opened. Billy and Ruth Graham came out and sat down right next to him. Billy Graham was saying to his friend Jim, "I'm committed to you. You can count on me. I'll be with you in the good times and I'll be with you in the tough times".

You can tell who your true friends are – not when everything's going great and not when you succeed – but when you fail and get off course. Stay committed to the people God has put in your life. Be loyal.

What was the result of Paul and Barnabas' commitment? The church expanded. The community grew stronger together and individual lives were changed. In Acts 16, we learn of a young Christian in Lystra (Timothy) and his mother. . Perhaps Timothy saw Paul being stoned firsthand in Lystra. It may be that it inspired him to devote his life to God after watching Paul's commitment and courage. He might have gone home that day with a resolve in his heart that he wanted to have the faith and courage that Paul had.

ENCOURAGEMENT MEANS BEING VULNERABLE

The day after the attempted public execution, Paul went to another city to encourage the church. His example of strength and boldness didn't stop there. After preaching in Derbe, he returned to the city that he was just stoned outside of to strengthen those people. Then he moved on to the city where the people who stoned him lived and encouraged the community there.

Many of us would call that reckless. Paul's life was in danger! What we see is that he found more value in ministering and loving the community than even in his own safety. Paul knew that he could make it through anything because the Holy Spirit was strengthening him.

Paul put himself in a vulnerable situation. While you may not fear being stoned to death, when you get serious about loving people you put yourself at risk.

Every relationship – whether with a spouse, parent, brother, sister, friend, or co-worker requires vulnerability.

Earlier we read that "love bears all things, believes all things, hopes all things, endures all things."

John Piper says:

> "To enter a relationship is to enter pain. And love is all over that. Love doesn't cop out. Love doesn't run away. Love doesn't throw in the towel. Love doesn't return evil for evil. Love endures and bears and comes back with kindness."[16]

Love doesn't say, "this far and no further." Love is not limited by what is reasonable or by what other people are willing to put up with. In no means am I saying that you should allow yourself to continually be hurt – physically or otherwise – by another person. Sometimes love bears pain from a safe and legal distance, but true love doesn't stop even when times are tough or someone is difficult to deal with.

► **Love is not limited by what is reasonable or by what other people are willing to put up with.**

SIMPLY THROUGH OUR WORDS

As Paul and Barnabas traveled, they were using their words to encourage people. I want to spend a little time on this point because this might be the most significant point of the chapter.

Your words are powerful.

The Bible says, "Death and life are in the power of the tongue."[17] Are you speaking words of love and encouragement, or words that tear people down? Your words get magnified – both for the good and the bad.

Encouragement is most often expressed through words. It is more than just trying to make somebody feel better.

When is the last time you've said something like this to someone?

- "Hang in there. You've got this."
- "It's really not as bad as you think."
- "I've been there. You're going to be fine."
- "You're not the only one who has faced this."
- "You are stronger than you think."
- "You've got this."

There is nothing inherently wrong with saying these things to someone, but biblical encouragement goes much deeper than making someone feel better in the moment. It's about speaking truth into their lives.

Paul said, "encourage one another and build one another up."[18] Biblical encouragement builds. If you've ever built a house or been a part of any kind of building project, you know that a structure needs solid building materials in order to stand. It also needs a solid foundation to stand upon. When encouraging someone, use words that are strong, not meaningless and empty. Avoid words that are meaningless or trite.

One of the best ways you can encourage somebody is by reminding them of the truth. Say things like:

- "You are a child of the most high God."
- "You have royal blood flowing through your veins."
- "The God who started a great work in you isn't finished yet."
- "God has not given you a spirit of fear."
- "God will keep you in perfect peace as you trust Him."
- "Your work will be rewarded one day."
- "God is the author and the finisher of your child's faith."

Let's take it one step further. A great way to boost the faith of someone you are trying to encourage is to personalize the promises of God for them. For example, speak Psalm 34:8 over a friend, "Lord, help Rebecca to taste and see that you Lord are good; bless her as she takes refuge in You."

Speak Deuteronomy 31:8 over your children by saying, "The Lord is going before Luci, Londyn, and Lily and will be with each of you; He will never leave you or forsake you. Girls, do not be afraid and do not be discouraged."

Encouraging others with your words is simple and it costs you nothing. Find ways to encourage those around you with your words.

> Encouraging others with your words is simple and it costs you nothing.

Go old school and pick up the phone. Call someone. Handwrite a card. Send flowers.

For those of you tech-savvy friends reading this, more than likely you are on email and social media every day. Use it to encourage people. More than half of the world now uses social media.[19] Social media, for all of its faults, isn't inherently bad. Platforms like Instagram, YouTube, Facebook, Twitter, TikTok, Pinterest, and Snapchat offer incredible opportunities to speak truth into people's lives. Use them to share Scripture, quotes, and stories that will "make for peace and the building up of one another."[20]

If you follow me on social media, you know that I devote a lot of time and attention to cheering on the community. I want to be good to people. I want every post to bless and encourage the people who see them. So before you create your next post, ask yourself, "Will this encourage the people who see it? Will it build them up? Am I speaking the truth?"

SIMPLY IN-COURAGE

When was the last time you encouraged someone? As you walk through life in a broken world, encouragement is an essential skill. Encouragement is like oxygen in the life of a community.

Rick Warren says:

> "It's not about you. The purpose of your life is far greater than your own personal fulfillment, your peace of mind, or even your happiness."[21]

If it's not about me, then it must be about you... and you... and you. Are you living your life for yourself or for others? Make it your life mission to live for others. There is an old hymn written by Charles D. Meigs in 1902 titled "Others." I memorized it in eighth grade.

Part of the hymn goes like this:

> Lord, help me live from day to day
> In such a self-forgetful way
> That even when I kneel to pray
> My prayer shall be for others.
>
> Yes, others, Lord, yes, others,
> Let this my motto be;
> Help me to live for others,
> That I may live like Thee.

I love those last two lines. Help me to live for others, that I may live like Thee. We have to learn to give ourselves away and live for others. When we do, the blessings of God will show up in our lives like never before.

This chapter has been about simple encouragement. We are going to do a play on words. Let's change encouragement to IN-couragement.

IN-couragement is about imparting something significant INTO another.

When you IN-courage someone, you place something INSIDE of them. You declare the truth of God's Word INTO their life. You show evidence of grace to help them see that God is using them. You share God's promises to remind them that God is in control. You speak courage to help them get through a difficult season. You state words of blessings to cheer them on, build them up, and strengthen them on the inside.

Proverbs says, "Anxiety in a man's heart weighs him down, but a good word makes him glad."[22] Your IN-couragement can speak the truth INTO hearts around you.

How do you IN-courage someone and build this "Christ with me" mentality that Paul Tripp talked about? It flows out of what Jesus is doing IN your own life. Because of Christ's work IN me, I can IN-courage those around me.

Choose to simply IN-courage.

▶ IN REAL LIFE
PRACTICAL WAYS TO SIMPLY ENCOURAGE

There isn't only one "right way" to encourage people. The sky's the limit. I know this for certain – it doesn't have to be "big." A small gesture can have a big impact. Here are a few practical ideas to help you get started.

1. Pray for greater love.
Ask God to give you a greater capacity to love people. The Apostle John said, "Beloved, let us love one another, for love is from God, and whoever loves has been born of God and knows God."[23] Ask God to bring someone to mind that you should reach out to.

2. Make encouragement a daily routine.
Personally commit to ongoing encouragement. For years, I have practiced my own 3-2-1 rule. I find 3 people to bless and encourage face-to-face. I send 2 texts with a word of encouragement. I call 1 person on the phone just to tell them I am thinking about them and praying for them. It's as simple as 1-2-3. At the beginning, I would put this on my calendar. Now it's a habit and part of my daily routine.

3. Be specific.
Being specific makes your encouragement more credible and concrete. If you see God at work in someone's life, share the evidence of grace with that person. Be specific. People are encouraged when they are reminded that God is at work in and through them.

4. Share Scripture.
The Bible is "alive and powerful."[24] The Bible is full of blessings and promises. When writing to the Christians at Rome, Paul referred to "the encouragement of the Scriptures" which give hope.[25]

5. Offer specific help.
Sometimes we need to give more than words. We need to give of our abilities and time to help in whatever way is needed. If you ask, "How can I help?" the person might be at a loss to answer. Ask, "Would it help if I..." or say, "I would like to..." Can you run an errand or get the grass mowed? What about dropping off some food or sending flowers to let someone know that you're thinking about them?

6. Smile.
A simple smile is a great way to encourage others. God is so good. Share his goodness through your smile. Proverbs reminds us that "A cheerful look brings joy to the heart."[26]

7. Be present.
Realize the power of presence. Just being with someone can be encouraging. When you're with others and give them your time and attention, you are telling them they are important.

8. Listen.
Ernest Hemingway said, "When people talk, listen completely. Most people never listen." The Bible tells us to be "quick to hear and slow to speak" not only in responding in anger[27] but in understanding the matters going on in someone's life.[28]

9. Do it right away.
If an encouraging thought comes to mind, speak it right then and there. It may not have the same effect if you wait. The

Bible says, "encourage one another daily, as long as it is called 'Today.'"[29]

10. Start now.

Who can you encourage right now? Who has blessed you recently that you can thank? What Scripture can you share with them? Giving encouragement doesn't have to be difficult, time-consuming, or a huge event. Just be sincere and watch God work.

American newspaper columnist George M. Adams once said "Encouragement is oxygen to the soul."[30] If you plan on making it through the day, you need oxygen. If you plan on fulling the purpose God has for your life, you need encouragement. The same is true for the people around you. Don't wait. Before you turn the page stop… pick one of these 10 ideas and go IN-courage someone!

CHAPTER 7
PRAISING THROUGH THE PAIN

Pain and suffering are constants in our world. Hurting people are everywhere. According to recent research, 76% of people have experienced at least one traumatic event in their lifetime. Across 14 types of adversities and traumas queried in the data, the most commonly experienced were sudden or premature death of a loved one, breakdown of a romantic relationship, or divorce/family breakdown.[1]

Maybe as you hold this book in your hands, you are in the middle of some serious pain. It might be a diagnosis, a broken heart, an unexpected text you weren't supposed to see, or a job loss. You know the right thing to do. You know God is with you. You know that you should trust Him. But it's not always easy.

When Pharaoh let the Israelites leave Egypt, Exodus 13 tells us that God did not lead them out by way of the coastal route. The Via Maris, known as "the way of the sea," was the shortest and most common way to travel from Egypt to Canaan. It had good and easy roads. It was the shortest distance. It was a trade route so it would be easy to buy food and water. It would have made sense to take that route. But God didn't lead them that way. God took them the long and hard way. The Via Maris was the road where Egypt's military outposts were. God anticipated dangers that they couldn't see ahead. He knew they weren't ready for the battles they would face.

Sometimes God uses difficult routes to prepare us for what's coming. When facing adversity, remember that it's not random or accidental. God has a purpose and He will use it for your good.

> When facing adversity, remember that it's not random or accidental.

Your best friend might stab you in the back. Your boss might pass you over and give the promotion to someone else. The business deal you've always dreamed of might fall through. Your prayer might not get answered the way you wanted it to. It's easy to get discouraged and think that God has forgotten about you… but He hasn't. He has a purpose.

The Bible says, "We know that for those who love God all things work together for good."[2] God won't allow adversity in your life unless He's going to use it for your good.

Kyle Idleman says:

> "Like the loving father who allows his child to get a painful vaccination shot, God allows pain because He knows it's for our greater good.
>
> - Perhaps God allows cancer to teach us to value what is eternal.
> - God may allow the difficult boss to teach us self-control.
> - God might allow unemployment to teach us faith.
> - God might allow a colicky baby to teach us patience.

He doesn't cause all things, but He does cause them to work together for our good. We come out on the other side of it looking a little more like Jesus."[3]

MOVEMENT CAUSES FRICTION

I learned in Junior High Science class that movement creates friction. What I didn't know at that time is how that principle applies to more than just physics. When things start moving the right direction in your life and God's favor shows up, expect some friction along the way.

Paul faced friction on his missionary journeys. The opposition primarily came from two places. First, the Jews in the towns he visited that didn't accept the message of Jesus would create problems. Secondly, his message would sometimes have a negative impact on businesses in the area which also created problems. The story I am about to share falls in that second category. We read about it in Acts 16.

Paul and Silas – two friends in real life – were ministering in Philippi. While in the city, a slave girl found them. This young girl was demon-possessed and was a source of money for her owners as a fortune teller. People would pay money and she would tell them what was going to happen in their lives. She kept following Paul and Silas everywhere they went and shouting, "These men are servants of the Most High God, who proclaim to you the way of salvation."[4] What she was saying was true and she continued doing this day after day.

At first Paul tolerated it, but he eventually grew irritated with the constant shouting. He didn't really appreciate the free advertising. Paul commanded the demonic spirit to come out of the girl and it immediately left. I can't imagine how good this must have felt for her. Talk about freedom! She was finally free from the demonic spirit.

TROUBLE IS COMING

Once her owners found out about this, they were not thrilled to say the least. Their source of income was gone. They started spreading lies about Paul and Silas and created quite a stir in town.

Order and control would have been important in a Roman military outpost like Philippi. There was an ongoing tension between the Roman government and the Jews anyway. So when the rioting crowd joined the slave girl's owners in accusing Paul and Silas of causing problems, the officials would have wanted to appease everyone and not let things get out of hand.

There were no legal charges made against Paul and Silas. They were simply accused of being troublemakers. We learn later in the story that the officials were planning on letting the crowd settle down and then early the next morning releasing them and sending them on their way.

They were stripped and severely beaten by the people. Jewish legal tradition gave a maximum number of blows that could be delivered when beating a person, but the Romans had no limit. All we know is that Paul and Silas were severely beaten. Paul later said, "I have worked much harder, been in prison more frequently, been flogged more severely, and been exposed to death again and again"[5]

After the horrible beating, they were imprisoned in maximum-security conditions. The jailer was instructed to watch them closely. They fastened their feet in the stocks. Stocks were large wood beams with an upper and lower section. Grooves were cut so that the prisoner's legs would be placed in it. Then the upper section was clamped down and fastened on the lower section. They would not be able to move and would be forced to remain in a sitting position.

Paul and Silas were humiliated by having their clothes torn from them, beaten with rods and whips, put into the darkness of a prison cell, and locked down by their legs fastened in stocks. This was an awful place to be. Yet, God was not far from them even in their trouble. Terrible situations set the stage for a miracle!

▶ Terrible situations set the stage for a miracle!

SETTING THE STAGE FOR A MIRACLE

Hours had passed. It was now about midnight.

Trials were heard by the officials mid-morning so they would not have to be outside during the heat of the day. This means Paul and Silas had been in chains for at least 12 hours. They felt the pain of the beatings and the discomfort of the stocks, yet they started praying and singing to God.

The Bible says, "About midnight Paul and Silas were praying and singing hymns to God, and the other prisoners were listening to them."[6] Although they had been arrested, beaten, and thrown into prison; they were filled with joy. They prayed and sang praises to God.

Tertullian said, "The legs feel nothing in the stocks when the heart is in heaven." It seemed as if nothing could make them stop praising God. Wounded and weary, beaten and bound, they prayed and sang praises to God. Think about how strange this would sound to the other prisoners. In the pitch dark of night, they heard Paul and Silas praying and singing. Those prison walls had probably never heard such a sound.

Then, out of nowhere, an earthquake shook the prison. Earthquakes were common in the region, but this one was supernatural. It was supernatural not only because of the timing and the location, but because of what happened. All the prison doors were opened and everyone's chains were broken. Now the prisoners could easily run and escape.

If the prisoners escaped then the jailer responsible would most likely have had to pay with his life. Realizing that this was probably going to happen, the jailer drew his sword to take his own life. But before he killed himself, Paul shouted out and told him to stop because they were still in the cell where they were before the earthquake.

When the jailer turned on the lights, he saw Paul and Silas and he fell down trembling. This was as dramatic as it sounds. He was more impacted by the love and joy demonstrated by Paul and Silas than by the earthquake itself.

WHAT MUST I DO TO BE SAVED?

Pause and get the picture of what was happening.

The guard was standing, poised, and ready to fall on his own sword. When someone is in a position like this, they are thinking about eternity.

He fell at their feet and asked, "Sirs, what must I do to be saved?"[7] He must have been listening to those prayers and hymns. The jailer was so impressed by the love and joy of Paul and Silas that he instantly wanted the kind of life that they had. This is how God wants our witness to be. We should be natural magnets drawing people to Jesus. Our lives should make others want what we have.

▶ We should be natural magnets drawing people to Jesus. Our lives should make others want what we have.

They replied, "Believe in the Lord Jesus, and you will be saved."[8] This is the essence of the Gospel. Salvation is by grace alone and received by faith alone. Paul did not send him to counseling. He didn't quiz him on theology. He didn't talk about church denominations. He simply pointed him to Jesus.

The same jailer who had very well beaten Paul and Silas earlier now trusted Jesus as his Lord and Savior. He washed their wounds and then took them to his house. They shared about Jesus with his family and they all believed and were baptized. Afterwards, they shared a meal together.

In the morning Paul revealed to the city officials the fact that he and Silas were Roman citizens. The officials had broken Roman law by beating Roman citizens publicly without a trial.

As time went on, the church was established in Philippi. Paul later wrote a letter to them that is all about joy. It's the New Testament book of Philippians.

WHAT WE LEARN ABOUT PAIN

Paul and Silas were following the Lord and doing the right thing, yet they experienced pain. Jesus said "it rains on the just and on the unjust." However, there is hope! David said, "The righteous person may have many troubles, but the LORD delivers him from them all."[9]

One day Paul said, "a wide door for effective work has opened to me, and there are many adversaries."[10] When God begins to open doors, opposition will follow. The enemy is not going to roll out the red carpet and make things easy for you.

Paul and Silas were mistreated and misunderstood. They experienced pain. Yet, they trusted the Lord. Here are some lessons we can learn from them.

1. REMEMBER, YOU'RE NOT ALONE.

Paul and Silas found themselves sitting in a dark prison cell – together.

When you find yourself facing adversity, remember that you're never alone. Others are fighting similar battles. You may not be suffering in physical proximity to someone else, but be assured you aren't alone in your pain.

There is an old proverb that tells about a man who had fallen into a hole and saw no way out. He hollered for help. Eventually, a rugged man walked by and upon hearing the man's plea and seeing his predicament, told the man that he needed to pick himself up by the bootstraps and find a way out on his own. Then he went on his way.

A holy man walked by and heard the man's desperate cry. He told him that he would say a prayer for him that he would find his way out and then scurried off.

Finally, an ordinary man walked by the hole and saw the first man and his situation. He listened to the man's plea for help. Then, without warning, the ordinary man jumped down into the hole with the first man.

"Why did you do that?" the first man asked.

The ordinary man replied, "Because I have been in this hole before, and I know the way out."

There are others who know the way out of the hole you find yourself in. You might not be able to get out of the financial hole you are in alone. You need a friend to get in the hole with you and help you get out. You might feel trapped in a toxic work environment. You need a friend to get in the hole with you and help you get out.

I've been humbled and amazed watching Beth – after 18 years of raising a daughter with special needs – get in the hole and selflessly love other families impacted by special needs. It hasn't always been easy, but she has allowed God to minister to her during this journey. As a result, she knows how to minister to others in their journey. She is kind, compassionate, and understanding. She knows when to encourage someone and she knows when to cry with someone. She knows when to speak up and when to be quiet and just listen.

You are not alone in the battle you are fighting. Leaning on others for help doesn't mean that you are weak. Asking for help is courageous and strong.

Ask God to bring people into your life to encourage you in your battle. Then be that encouragement to someone else. Be willing to get in the hole.

> Ask God to bring people into your life to encourage you in your battle. Then be that encouragement to someone else.

Rick Warren said:

> "I can't tell you how many people my wife and I have been able to help since our son Matthew died several years ago. People who struggle with mental illness and the grief of losing a child came out of the woodwork because they needed encouragement and hope. With God's grace, we've been able to help others who are in pain, even as we carry our own deep hurt. Because of this, God has given us purpose in our pain and helped many people to move forward in healing. God can use your pain, too, to help others struggling with the same pain."[11]

The shortest verse in the Bible is, "Jesus wept."[12] Jesus wept when he heard that his friend Lazarus had died. Why did He do this when He knew He was going to raise Lazarus back to life soon? He wept because He allowed Himself to get in the hole with the people around Him. You can do the same. The Bible says, "Bear one another's burdens, and so fulfill the law of Christ."[13] This is what friends in real life do.

2. FIND GOD'S PRESENCE IN THE PAIN.

While hurting, bleeding, and chained in a dark prison cell; you would think that Paul and Silas would retreat into depression or bitterness. You would think that they would start asking God "Why me?" Instead, they did the unthinkable. They started praying and praising God.

Nothing shows our spiritual maturity more than staying calm when everything around us says to stress out. Paul and Silas had no control over what was happening on the outside, but they could control what was happening on the inside.

I'm sure that when they were arrested, stripped of their clothing, beaten by the people, and ordered to be thrown into prison; that they had been praying and asking God for help. Even though they may have thought that God didn't hear them earlier, they kept talking to Him through the night. They still trusted Him. They knew that God was right there with them even in their pain.

Joseph knew God was with him in his pain. One day he found himself being falsely accused and thrown into prison. The Bible says, "the LORD was with Joseph" in prison.[14]

David believed that God was with him in the middle of his affliction. He said, "I will rejoice and be glad in your steadfast love, because you have seen my affliction; you have known the distress of my soul."[15]

God is always with you. He is with you in times of peace and in times of trouble. The secret is to keep your mind on Him. Isaiah said, "You keep him in *perfect peace* whose mind is stayed on you, because he trusts in you."[16] (italics mine) This is such an incredible promise. In Hebrew, the term "perfect peace" is actually *shalom shalom*. In the Hebrew language, repetition communicates intensity. It isn't just *shalom*; it is *shalom shalom* – perfect peace!

Cynthia Heald writes:

> "It is in steadfastly fixing your thoughts on God and trusting and abandoning yourself to the Lord that you will be kept in perfect peace. How incredibly gracious of God to bless you with His deep, abiding peace. The peace imparted by the Lord is peace that takes away the strain and stress. Jesus has overcome the world and He calms the storms. All He asks is our trust and our time to hear His voice."[17]

Later, Paul would write this to the community in Philippi: "Do not be anxious about anything, but in everything by prayer and supplication with thanksgiving let your requests be made known to God. And the peace of God, which surpasses all understanding, will guard your hearts and your minds in Christ Jesus."[18]

I read a story about an old lady who was walking along the road carrying a heavy basket. A man driving in a carriage invited her to ride with him. She got into the carriage, but left the basket on her lap. The man asked why she didn't set it down on the floor of the carriage. She answered, "I am heavy enough myself! I don't want to make the load heavier by putting the basket down."

Seems crazy, but how often do we do the same thing?

God is present in your trouble. He is strong enough to carry both you and your pain. You don't have to carry it yourself.

My mom had a prayer that she kept on our refrigerator door when I was growing up called "Footprints in the Sand." It goes like this:

> One night I dreamed a dream. I was walking along the beach with my Lord. Across the dark sky flashed scenes from my life. For each scene, I noticed two sets of footprints in the sand, one belonging to me and one to my Lord.
>
> When the last scene of my life shot before me I looked back at the footprints in the sand. There was only one set of footprints. I realized that this was at the lowest and saddest times of my life. This always bothered me and I questioned the Lord about my dilemma.
>
> "Lord, You told me when I decided to follow You, You would walk and talk with me all the way. But I'm aware that during the most troublesome times of my life there is only one set of footprints. I just don't understand why, when I need You most, You leave me."
>
> He whispered, "My precious child, I love you and will never leave you, never, ever, during your trials and testings. When you saw only one set of footprints, it was then that I carried you."

God is very near to you today. It may feel like you are walking alone, but you aren't really alone. He knows about the pain you are carrying and the trouble around you. He hears every prayer. Just like He was with Paul and Silas in that prison cell, He is with you wherever you find yourself. There is a presence beside you and protection all around you.

3. TURN UP THE PRAISE.

The enemy wants to keep you from remembering how good God is because he knows it's one of the secrets to a breakthrough.

Paul and Silas had every right to be down. They were locked in prison, which back then was more like the resemblance of a dungeon. It was a dark, damp, stench-ridden place, with no facility for waste and no comforts of any kind. They were fastened in stocks which caused cramps and a loss of circulation.

In spite of the throbbing pain in their bodies and the horrible surroundings, Paul and Silas were "praying and singing hymns to God."[19] What a strange sound this must have been to the other prisoners, who were used to hearing the groans or cursings of the prisoners who had been beaten.

It's easy to praise God when things are going well and you're on the mountain top. It takes faith and maturity to praise Him in the pain.

> It takes faith and maturity to praise Him in the pain.

We know what happened to Paul and Silas. "All the prison doors flew open, and everyone's chains came loose." Every door opened. Every chain broke. All because they prayed and sang praises to God.[20]

Maybe you need a breakthrough in your life. Is there a door that you need opened? Chains that you need broken? It's time to turn up the praise!

The Bible says that God inhabits the praises of His people.[21] In other words, He dwells in the atmosphere of His praise. Praise is more than a response from coming into His presence. Praise is a vehicle that takes you into His presence!

Paul later told the Philippians to present their needs to God "by prayer and supplication with thanksgiving."[22] It's easy to get so consumed in what you need that your time with God ends up sounding like a complaining session. You're just telling God everything that's wrong and everything you need. While it's okay to talk to God about your needs, you should also take time to praise Him. He is worthy!

I read a story about a missionary who had contracted smallpox before there was a vaccine. At that time it was quite often fatal. This missionary began praying to the Lord regarding her sickness, when the Lord gave her a vision of an old-fashioned balance scale. One side was labeled "Prayer" and the other "Praise." She noticed in the vision that the "Prayer" side was stacked up high, while the "Praise" side had just a small stack, causing that side to sit way up high. The scale was out of balance.

The Lord spoke to her and said, "When your praises equal your prayers, you will be healed." She spent two days doing nothing but praising God. She had a lot of catching up to do! During this time she didn't ask God for anything – she simply praised Him. At the end of those two days, she was completely healed. That's the power of praise!

Do your praises equal your prayers? Is your scale balanced? Don't wait to offer praise and thanks to God until things are just as you'd like them to be. Start praising Him now. Praise Him for who He is and what He's done in your life.

Paul and Silas could have spent the night talking about how big their problems were. Instead they chose to talk about how big their God was. And what happened? God opened the doors and broke the chains!

4. PREPARE FOR SOMETHING NEW AND BETTER.

Paul said, "*We rejoice* in our sufferings, knowing that suffering produces *endurance*, and endurance produces *character*, and character produces *hope*."[23] (emphasis mine) As you endure suffering, you grow and change. You find joy. You learn to endure. You build character. You discover hope.

It's so interesting that three words Paul used in association with suffering are joy, hope, and patience. These are three fruits of the Holy Spirit. Let God use your pain to develop the fruits of the Spirit in your life and make you everything He has created you to be.

Sometimes it takes suffering to bring out the best in you. One way that the Holy Spirit molds and shapes you is through pain. Growth often means pain. And growth without pain is an oxymoron.

> Growth often means pain.
> And growth without pain is an oxymoron.

One of the most difficult things about pain is the feeling that it's pointless. When you're a kid and you have growing pains, at least you always have something to show for it. You get teeth. You grow taller. The pain is necessary to make way for the new. When you have spiritual growing pains, God is making way for something new and better.

There's a story about two miners who lived in a cabin on a mountainside. There had been many rich mines on this mountain. However, time had passed and they were pretty well emptied out and were being abandoned one by one. All the other miners were packing up and going home. These two were about ready to abandon their cabin when one night it caught on fire and burned to ashes. A short time later it was discovered that this cabin had been sitting on a rich outcropping of valuable ore. It wasn't until the cabin had been lost that the hidden treasure was revealed.

The adversities and troubles in life often hide treasures you would never find otherwise. You find new strength. You find new hope. You find new friends. You find a new message to share with others.

As Joyce Meyer writes:

> "We have to let God take us through things and let Him work in us so our mess becomes our message. Difficult things that we have endured in our past prepare us for God's blessings in our future."[24]

Your mess can become your message!

In Psalms it says, "We went through fire and flood, but you brought us to a place of great abundance."[25] Everybody wants to be in the place of abundance, but we don't want what it takes to get there. Notice you have to go through the fire and through the flood to get to the place of abundance.

In the Gospel of John, Jesus speaks of Himself as the vine and His people as branches of that vine. "Every branch that does bear fruit He prunes, that it may bear more fruit."[26]

How are vines pruned? The gardener goes into the vineyard and prunes the vines, often cutting away such a large portion of them that it looks like they have been destroyed. But they aren't destroyed. On the contrary, they produce a more abundant harvest; much more abundant than would have been possible had they not been pruned so thoroughly.

Have you trusted Jesus as your Lord and Savior? If so, you are a branch in Christ. As a branch, don't think it's going to all be smooth and easy. God wants you to bear an abundance of fruit. You can't do that when you are comfortable. Sometimes there's a pruning.

Jesus is a good gardener. He won't let adversity prune you too closely. But He also won't remove that which will make you better. Like Paul and Silas, learn to rejoice in your suffering, knowing God is using it to produce in you what you could not produce in yourself.

5. WATCH FOR OPPORTUNITIES.

People watch with great interest whenever Christians face adversity. How will they respond when hardships come? When they lose loved ones? When they get a bad medical report? When they lose their job?

Others are watching to see if your faith is genuine. They watch to see if you are going to stay down, resort to bitterness, or give up on God.

Paul and Silas had good reasons to be down on life, but they knew that God was up to something good. They knew that He had beauty for those ashes. They knew that their problems presented great opportunities.

In that prison cell, Paul and Silas "were praying and singing hymns to God, *and the prisoners were listening to them.*"[27] (italics mine)

The prisoners were listening. I'm sure the jailer was listening, as well. But they weren't just listening, they were watching. Once the doors were opened and their chains broken, Paul and Silas stayed in their cell when they could have easily made a run for the door. Their actions affected other prisoners and the jailer. The jailer wanted what Paul and Silas had and went on to trust Jesus as his Lord and Savior.

In the same way, there are people watching you right now. They're developing an opinion about God based on your life. The Bible says that you are "an epistle written in our hearts, known and read of all men... written not with ink, but with the Spirit of the living God."[28] You are the only Bible that some people ever will read. Others are watching you. The way you handle pain can impact their lives.

> Others are watching you. The way you handle pain can impact their lives.

I read the following poem by an unknown author.

> I am my neighbor's Bible:
> He reads me when we meet,
> Today he reads me in my house,
> Tomorrow in the street;
> He may be relative or friend,
> Or slight acquaintance be;
> He may not even know my name,
> Yet he is reading me.

Don't waste your pain. God will open opportunities for you in the hard times that you would not have otherwise. The Bible says, "Better is the end of a thing than its beginning."[29] I want you to hear this from me: Better is the end! Keep your eyes on what's coming.

One of my favorite stories in the Bible is that of Joseph.[30] God didn't cause the problems in Joseph's life, but He stayed with him every step of the way and turned those difficulties into opportunities. Eventually, Joseph became the second in command in all of Egypt and saved many people from dying from a famine. God always has a purpose in our pain.

David Jeremiah wrote:

> "What do Paul's letters to the Ephesians, Philippians, Colossians, and Philemon; the book of Revelation, John Bunyan's Pilgrim's Progress and A Discourse Touching Prayer, Dietrich Bonhoeffer's Letters and Papers from Prison, and Martin Luther's translation of the New Testament all have in common? They were all written while the authors were in prison or in exile. Would they have been written otherwise? We don't know. But we do know these men of God didn't miss the opportunity to capitalize on the moment. Problems represent opportunities for those who embrace them."[31]

Don't waste your pain. Those problems represent opportunities! Allow God to help you. Then help others. Here is how I found that God works. We experience adversity. God ministers to us. Then we minister to others in the way that God ministered to us.

God said in Psalm 50, "Call upon Me in the day of trouble; I will deliver you, and you shall glorify Me."[32] He didn't say, "Call on Me and I'll keep you from trouble." He said, "Call on Me when you're in trouble." You can call on God. He is there with you.

I read a story about two young college students who were traveling to Kenya to work on a mission project. They were in their early 20's and both former college basketball players. They had prayed that everything would go smoothly, but when the plane tried to land in London it was too foggy and they missed their connecting flight.

They were disappointed as they had to spend the night in the airport. The only seats they had on the next flight were up front in first class. About midway through the flight, the plane took a nosedive and started heading straight toward the ground. People were panicking and screaming. It looked like they were going to die. These young men heard noise in the cockpit. It sounded like a struggle. This was pre-9/11 when you could go up into the cockpit. They opened the door to find that a deranged man had taken control of the plane. The pilots were trying to pull him off but they were very small and couldn't budge him. These guys were both over 6' 6". They were big and strong. They grabbed the man, ripped him off the controls, and tied him up.

One of the young men later said, "There were literally hundreds of people back home praying for us, knowing we were going on this mission trip. There was this strength within that made me get up and go. It came from God."[33]

The plane had descended from 30,000 feet to 4,000 feet. Within another minute or two, they would have all been killed. That delay in London seemed like a bad thing, but really it was good. They couldn't see it at the time. They didn't like it, and it didn't fit into their plans; but God held them back on purpose so they could save that whole plane. Sometimes God will use your pain to help somebody else.

Don't give up. One day God told Isaiah, "See, *I am doing a new thing*! Now it springs up; do you not perceive it? I am making a way in the wilderness and streams in the wasteland."[34] (italics mine) This is your new day. He's about to open doors you never dreamed would open!

Remember the words of C.S. Lewis, "Hardships often prepare ordinary people for an extraordinary destiny." God is about to use your pain to create some new opportunities for you. People around you are going to see the goodness of God on your life like never before!

> God is about to use your pain to create some new opportunities for you.

▶IN REAL LIFE
10 PRACTICAL WAYS TO HELP A FRIEND WHO'S HURTING

Ecclesiastes says, "If one falls down, the other helps, But if there's no one to help, tough!"[35] If you have a friend who's hurting, be a good friend and help. It doesn't have to be complicated. Here are some practical ways you can help:

1. Pray for them.
There is power in prayer. When we pray, we invite God to come into the problem and to do His supernatural work.

2. Read the Bible together.
God's Word is medicine to your soul. It heals from the inside out. As Joyce Meyer says, "It's important to remember that the Lord is our Healer, and that His Word is our medicine."[36]

3. Send a card of encouragement.
It's nice to get something in the mail that isn't junk or a bill. Send a card of encouragement. Encouragement means "to impart courage." It's crazy how something as simple as a card can do that.

4. Don't play savior.
You don't have to rush in with solutions and advice. You don't need to be the fixer or the savior. It's okay to be silent and allow the Holy Spirit to work.

5. Be with them.
Grief and pain can feel very lonely. Your presence can make all the difference. Don't worry about saying the wrong things.

Many times just your physical presence of being there for someone makes all the difference.

6. Send a text.
Texts don't take long to send, but can come just at the right time. Your encouraging words just might help them come out stronger on the other side.

7. Call them.
Take a minute to call and check in. Offer to help. Instead of saying, "Let me know if you need anything," make a specific offer like, "I can bring pizza by tomorrow night if you'd like."

8. Include them.
Include them in your activities. Invite them over to eat. They might not come, but they will know you care.

9. Help in practical ways.
When someone is hurting, even little things can be overwhelming. Wash their car. Mow the grass. Watch their kids. Run errands for them. Organize a meal train. Clean their house. Do something practical.

10. Be patient.
People's needs are rarely resolved overnight. Keep showing up. Keep being the hands and feet of Jesus to your friend in need.

Helping a friend who is hurting isn't always easy. Entering into someone else's pain can be uncomfortable, but with God's help you can do it. The Bible says that just as Christ has comforted us… we can comfort others.[37]

CHAPTER 8
IT'S A TEAM SPORT

In high school, I fried fish at Long John Silvers. I started for the gas money and stayed for the free hush puppies. While working at Long Johns, I found that many of my friends were people who worked there, too.

Fast forward to college and I was a closing manager at Fazolis. I found that many of my friends at the time worked at Fazolis, as well.

After college, I picked up golf for a few years. Guess who some of my closest friends were at the time? Other guys in my church whom I golfed with.

This is how friendships work. They are often based on similarities and mutual interests. Today, I find that my closest friends are other pastors and entrepreneurs. As great as these friends are, my dearest friends are those that I can call and pray with. They are friends who I talk "Bible" with.

Pat is one such friend. He is an electrical lineman that loves the Lord. Our girls are friends and play sports together. Almost every time that Pat and I talk, the conversation moves to the Bible. Pat will text me and ask me to read a passage of Scripture. He will follow up by asking what the Holy Spirit said to me because he wants to know if He said the same thing to both of us. Pat is a real life friend and a great encouragement.

Hebrews says, "let us consider how to stir up one another to love and good works, not neglecting to meet together, as is the habit of some, but encouraging one another, and all the more as you see the Day drawing near."[1] I've mentioned this passage of Scripture several times so far in this book. What I haven't mentioned is what makes it so powerful.

The twenty three verses leading up to Hebrews 10:24-25 is what makes it so powerful. It talks about the amazing sacrifice that Jesus made for us on the cross. We learn how He made a single sacrifice for our sins, entered into the most holy place with His blood, and forever wiped the slate clean of our sins. We now have access to God because of His great sacrifice on the cross.

After sharing these incredible truths, the author of Hebrews says, "Let's stir one another up to love and good works. Let's encourage each other. Let's help each other out. Let's meet together. " Because of Jesus, you have full access to God. As a result, you should help the community around you grow closer to Him.

> Because of Jesus, you have full access to God. As a result, you should help the community around you grow closer to Him.

The Old Testament prophet Daniel and his friends, Shadrach, Meshach, and Abednego, went through a lot together. They were pretty much kidnapped from their homes in Jerusalem during a siege by King Nebuchadnezzar of Babylon. One of the first things that the new King did was change their names, hoping that they would forever forget the God of their fathers. While in the king's training program, they took a big risk by not accepting his food and drink because they didn't want to defile themselves. They faced numerous other tests and trials. Through it all, they stood toe-to-toe with each other; finding courage and strength as together they were dedicated to God and His Word. This is the power of friends in real life.

As much as it pains me to admit it, I've never been a good basketball player. It pains me because my dad was a basketball legend in his day and holds several NCCAA records. My basketball career consisted of 5th and 6th grade basketball camps and pre-season 7th grade basketball. I say pre-season because I quit before we ever played our first game. There was a kid on our team that bullied me around and on top of that we had a coach with an out of control temper. I didn't like either of them so I quit and gave up on my basketball career.

As a kid, I would rarely shoot the basketball because I lacked confidence. I'm a few years older now with a daughter that loves to shoot baskets with me in the driveway. Even though I'd like to think I am more confident, I am still a pretty lousy shot.

If I wanted to, I could make it my mission in life to get better at the game. I could spend a few hours a day shooting free throws. I could find a trainer that would help me handle the ball better and make three pointers. That would no doubt improve my skills, but I'd be in for a rude awakening the next time I got back in a 5-on-5 game. While my personal skills would have improved, adding teammates and defenders changes everything. You have to learn to work with your teammates. You've got to pass and set screens. Having opponents trying to stop you from taking good shots and putting you on the defensive is a totally different scenario than shooting free throws and making layups in the driveway.

The point of basketball is not to be really good at shooting baskets on your own. It's about teaming up with four other people to defeat five opponents. It's a team sport. In the same sense, to win at life and make a difference, you can't go at it alone. You need a team.

A MINOR ROLE BUT A MAJOR STORY

Built at the foot of Mount Vermio sits the city of Veria. It overlooks the Macedonian Plain, which was the heart of the Macedonian Empire. It is an incredibly beautiful view. Veria was the first city in Macedonia to be conquered by the Romans. A few insignificant ruins from the Greek and Roman periods are scattered throughout the area.

Today, 30,000 people live in this ancient city, through which streams of water flow along its streets. Water has had a prevalent influence on the town because of its abundance. In fact, that's how the city got its name.[2]

Most of us would recognize this city by a much different name than Veria. The Bible mentions its name only a few times, but most Christians remember it because of how they treated the Word of God. In New Testament times, the town's name was Berea.

The Berean Church was visited by Paul somewhere between 70 and 90 AD. Though their interaction was brief, it was important enough to be recorded in the Bible. They have a minor role in the whole of the Bible, but their impact is huge.

Acts tells their story:

> "The brothers immediately sent Paul and Silas away by night to Berea, and when they arrived they went into the Jewish synagogue. Now these Jews were more noble than those in Thessalonica; they received the word with all eagerness, examining the Scriptures daily to see if these things were so. Many of them therefore believed, with not a few Greek women of high standing as well as men."[3]

In this chapter, I'm going to encourage you to find some real life friends that you can diligently study the Bible with. A lot of people have God in a Sunday morning box. That's when they come to church to worship, pray, and open their Bibles. Then they spend the rest of their week with all of their non-church friends talking about everything but the Bible.

They love God. They love the Bible. But the Bible seldom intersects with their relationships. As a result, they miss so much of the favor and blessings God would have for them.

If you have grown up in the church or spent much time listening to Bible teaching, you can't think about being diligent with the Scriptures without thinking about the Jews in Berea. In fact, a lot of churches (mine included) have had Bible study groups called "The Bereans" for this very reason. The Bereans are a shining example of faithfulness to the Word of God in community and give us great inspiration on how we can influence the culture around us.

INFLUENCING THE CULTURE AROUND US

Before we talk about what took place in Berea, it's worth taking the time to understand what happened leading up to this event. Paul and Silas had been ministering in the city of Thessalonica. However, their message was not met with enthusiasm to say the least. The Bible says that "other Jews were jealous; so they rounded up some bad characters from the marketplace, formed a mob, and started a riot in the city. They rushed to Jason's house in search of Paul and Silas in order to bring them out to the crowd."[4]

The Jews were upset because they were losing the war that was going on between them and the new Christians. This wasn't a physical war, but a spiritual one which led to persecution of the Christians.

Many Christians sense a similar war happening in our culture today. It's not physical but spiritual. While the culture looks different today, the battle over truth is still there. Evidence of this battle is all around us as Satan does everything he can to lead people away from God's truth.

I am reminded of a story I read recently about Adolph Hitler. As his hunger for power grew, his army marched across Europe. In some cases, the fight could hardly be called a battle. The German army advanced, with its tanks and with technologically advanced weapons. In some of the underdeveloped nations, their armies made a futile effort to resist Hitler's aggression, fighting back with spears and even rocks. However, it was no contest at all because they weren't equipped for the battle.

The same could be said of Satan and those whom he opposes today. So many people don't even know there is a spiritual war going on. It's important that you understand Satan's schemes, the weapons he uses, and also the weapons which God has provided for your defense.

> It's important that you understand Satan's schemes, the weapons he uses, and also the weapons which God has provided for your defense.

Ephesians 6:10-20 gives us the clearest definition of the spiritual war that exists in our culture. It not only assures us that there is a spiritual war, but it warns us that apart from utilizing the weapons which God has provided for us – including His Word – we are hopelessly underpowered.

In 1975, Loren Cunningham (founder of Youth With a Mission) and Bill Bright (founder of Campus Crusade for Christ) had lunch together in Colorado. Both men had been given a dream by God that contained a message to give to the other. That message was about the "Seven Mountains" of influence. Theologian Francis Schaeffer received a similar message from the Lord at about the same time. All three men believed that in order for the church to impact the world for Jesus Christ, the church would need to influence the "Seven Mountains" of culture.

The idea is really quite simple. In our culture there are "Seven Mountains" (think of them as "spheres" or simply "areas" of influence) and the church is called to build influence on each of those mountains. These "Seven Mountains" influence the way a culture thinks and behaves. They are:

- Business
- Government
- Media
- Arts and Entertainment
- Education
- The Family
- Religion

God was telling these men where the battlefield was. It was on these "Seven Mountains" where culture is won or lost and where spiritual battles are most often fought. I am not going to take the time to unpack each of these "Seven Mountains." You know what they are and I am sure you agree that they each heavily influence our society. I'm also sure you'll agree with me that there is a battle over truth in each of these areas.

If we are to be change agents in our culture, then we must engage these "Seven Mountains" of influence as a Christian community. But how? How do we build influence on each of those mountains? I believe we can learn some valuable lessons from the community at Berea.

A COMMUNITY THAT WAS DIFFERENT...
AND MADE A DIFFERENCE

As I said earlier, the Jews were angry and jealous because they were losing the spiritual war with the new Christians. In Thessalonica, they were so angry that they got some "bad characters" to stir things up as the ESV puts it. The NASV is more forceful and says that these were wicked men. The NKJV says they were evil men. These guys went after Paul and Silas with such vengeance that they had to get out of town as quickly as possible.

They escaped the Jews in Thessalonica and went straight to Berea. Once there, Paul's first stop was the Jewish synagogue. He didn't do this to agitate the Jews, though that certainly happened. Paul was a Jew himself and he felt the need to reach out to God's chosen people who were his own people as well. He had a burden in his heart to share his story and to see the Jews come to faith in Jesus themselves.

Once there, Paul found that the Jews in Berea were much different than the Jews in Thessalonica. The book of Acts tells us:

> "Now these Jews were more noble than those in Thessalonica; they received the word with all eagerness, examining the Scriptures daily to see if these things were so. Many of them therefore believed, with not a few Greek women of high standing as well as men."[5]

Berea was about 45 miles from Thessalonica to the southwest. Although they were close in proximity to the Jews in Thessalonica, they were vastly apart in how they approached the Scriptures. They teach us some great lessons on building influence on the "Seven Mountains" of our society.

START BY BEING KIND.

The Bereans were "*more noble* than those in Thessalonica."[6] (italics mine) The Greek word for "noble" is *eugenesteroi*. It meant "well born" and implied nobility. A noble person is someone who shows personal qualities that people admire. It describes someone who is kind, has a generous spirit, and is open-minded toward truth. It is someone who is not prejudiced, hostile, or suspicious of others. This describes the Bereans.

If you are going to positively impact your community and the culture at large, it will require kindness. Resist the temptation to get angry, use sarcasm, or make derogatory comments and you'll have a much better chance of being a positive influence on people.

Proverb says, "A word of encouragement works wonders."[7] So often we look around our workplace and in our communities and beg God to do wonders... but what if those wonders are in our kind words? Don't discount the power of being kind. It can literally work wonders.

I've read about a three-year-old little boy named Michael. His mother, Karen, had just found out that she was pregnant with a little girl. Like any good mother, when she found out that another baby was on the way, she did what she could to help her son prepare for a new sibling.

The new baby was going to be a girl, and day after day Michael sang to his sister in mommy's tummy. He was building a bond of love with his little sister before he even met her. He was so excited and couldn't wait to see his little sister. All through the day, Michael would come over to his mommy's tummy and sing, "You are my sunshine, my only sunshine". Week after week, month after month, hundreds of times he kept singing.

The mother finally went into labor. There were complications with the delivery and she had to be rushed to the operating room for an emergency c-section. Unfortunately, the baby didn't respond well. She was alive, but doctors told the parents there was very little chance she would survive.

The days inched by and the little girl got worse. The pediatrician had to tell the parents there was very little hope and to prepare for the worst. Karen and her husband contacted a local cemetery about a burial plot. They had prepared a nursery in their home for their new baby and now they found themselves planning a funeral.

The baby was taken to the neonatal intensive care unit. Michael kept asking, "When can I see my baby sister?" Several days went by and word came that the baby would probably not make it through the night. The mother knew that if Michael didn't see his sister that night he may not ever see her alive.

When the head nurse wasn't watching, she snuck Michael into intensive care. He was taken back by all the tubes and monitors on his little sister. The head nurse saw him and yelled, "Get that boy out of here now. No children are allowed."

Without his mother saying a word, Michael started singing, "You are my sunshine, my only sunshine. You make me happy when skies are gray." Instantly the baby girl seemed to respond. Her pulse rate began to calm down and became steady. The nurse looked at little Michael and said, "Keep singing!"

As he kept singing, the nurse watched in amazement as the baby's heart rate became normal. Her blue color began to go away. Instead of being shaky and jittery, there was a calmness over the baby. It was like those words from a 5-year-old boy were releasing healing and wholeness into his baby sister. Against all odds, the baby got better. Today she is perfectly healthy and whole.

Proverbs says, "Kind words are like honey— sweet to the soul and healthy for the body." Your kind words are powerful! They are powerful enough to release healing and wholeness.

> Your kind words are powerful! They are powerful enough to release healing and wholeness.

There's an interesting theory called the butterfly effect. It describes how the flap of a butterfly's wing can lead to a cyclone in another part of the world. It is a mathematical construct that explains how small changes can have large consequences. So it is with kindness. A single, simple kind act can have enormous consequences.

Proverbs says "What is desirable in a person is his kindness."[8] You'll never positively influence the culture by being mean, inconsiderate, and harsh. Instead, be kind. Choose to be mindful of the needs of others.

In the parable of the Good Samaritan, the Samaritan saw the needs of the beaten man on the road and he sacrificed his time and resources to serve his needs. The Samaritan didn't do this to be seen by others or to get anything from the injured man. He was noble. He was kind. He made a difference. And we still talk about him today.

START LISTENING.

In addition to being kind and noble, the Bereans "received the word with all eagerness."[9] The Greek word for eagerness is *prothumos*, which suggests that they listened with enthusiasm and zeal. They didn't think they had all the answers. I visualize them literally leaning in with their hands cupped behind their ears listening intently to every single word from Paul.

We live in a world where everyone wants to talk, but nobody wants to listen. Everybody wants to be understood. Few want to understand.

> Everybody wants to be understood.
> Few want to understand.

If you are going to positively influence the "Seven Mountains" of culture, it requires active listening. Jesus' half brother said, "Let every person be quick to hear, slow to speak."[10] The skill of listening is incredibly rare. We have the ability to run our mouths more than ever before. That's because we don't have to run our mouths with our actual mouths. We have devices that we carry in our pockets. We can each be keyboard warrior extraordinaires where we share our deepest thoughts and profound opinions right at our fingertips.

Sometimes we just need to be quiet and listen... even to people we may not agree with. Don't text. Don't tweet. Don't go live on Facebook. Don't post online. Just listen.

That's not to say there aren't times to be loud. There are. God has left you as an ambassador for the Lord Jesus Christ in your sphere of influence. But be careful not to undermine your influence and credibility by getting angry, dominating conversations, or forcing your opinion on others. This is rarely effective. Instead, be kind and listen. If you do, when you actually speak the truth it will mean something.

Winston Churchill once said, "Courage is what it takes to stand up and speak; courage is also what it takes to sit down and listen."

Jesus commanded us, "Consider carefully how you listen." Listening is not a passive activity. It is more than being quiet and letting someone else speak. It requires full attention, focused concentration, and careful thinking.

Friends, we are all talking. Probably more than we should. Let's make sure that our words are "full of grace and seasoned with salt."[11] Let's also make sure we are known as people who really listen.

GET IN THE BIBLE YOURSELF

When Paul arrived in Berea, he found a community that was eager to study the Scriptures. "...they received the word with all eagerness, examining the Scriptures daily to see if these things were so."[12]

You can just feel the excitement that they must have had. I can see them hearing something new about Jesus from Paul, whispering to each other enthusiastically, and then promptly sending someone to get another scroll from Isaiah to pour over as Paul is teaching to see if what he was saying was true.

To have heard that Jesus was the Messiah would have been incredibly shocking to the Jews. A coming Messiah had been prophesied for generations and generations, and now someone was claiming that He had appeared… and in their lifetime!

President Ronald Reagan famously said, "Trust, but verify." When Paul talked about Jesus Christ, the Messiah, and His church; the Bereans trusted, but then verified and checked it out for themselves to make sure it was accurate. I wish I could have been there firsthand to see the joy and excitement that followed when they realized that Jesus was indeed the Messiah that they had been waiting for.

The Bereans loved studying the Word of God. It wasn't a chore; it was something that they were excited about doing. Have you come to this same point in your life? The Bible is no ordinary book.

Chuck Swindoll says,

> "News articles may inform us. Novels may inspire us. Poetry may enrapture us. But only the living, active Word of God can transform us."

Beth and I own 17 acres of woods a mile down the road from our home. We enjoy taking walks and ATV rides back on the property. We especially like just stopping and gazing at the amazing, tall trees. They are literally breath-taking. You know what each of these trees have in common? They have deep roots.

Joni Eareckson Tada says:

> "The branches of growing trees not only reach higher, but their roots grow deeper. It's impossible for a strong tree to have high branches without having deep roots. It would become top-heavy and topple over in the wind. The same is true with Christians. It's impossible for us to grow in the Lord without entwining our roots around His Word and deepening our life in His commands."[13]

The Bible often describes godly people as trees. If you want to be a tall, immovable tree, it will require deep roots which comes from time spent in God's Word.

Beth's grandfather used to preach, "What you do with the Bible determines what God does with you." If you want to influence the "Seven Mountains" of our culture, you need to be rooted in the Word of God. There is a battle over what is right and what is wrong in each of these seven areas.

> What you do with the Bible determines what God does with you.

Are you trying to help your children form a biblical worldview? Do you feel like you are on the front lines of a spiritual battle at work? Do you feel the polarization between opposing sides when it comes to hot topics in our culture? Do you struggle with how to respond to increasingly anti-Christian sentiment in our media?

Too often, when push comes, shove follows. In other words, when culture opposes what we believe to be true, we immediately feel the need to give it back. We adopt an "all's fair in love and war" mindset. After all, in a war you don't turn the other cheek. You strike back as hard, or harder, than your opponent. That's how wars are won. But is that how spiritual wars are won?

A better approach is to be noble. Be kind. Listen more than you talk. Study the Bible so that you know what you believe and why you believe it.

Yes, be ready to give an answer for your faith, but first get serious about loving your enemies. Start praying for those who are blinded to the truth. Remember the second greatest commandment according to Jesus is "You shall love your neighbor as yourself."[14] This includes those who don't agree with you. Win them with love.

The champion of winning people with love is Bob Goff. I love what he said in one of his books:

> "If you ask a thousand people who don't want anything to do with religion why that is, they'll tell you all the reasons they don't like it, but I doubt they'd be describing the real stuff. They'll describe a guy or a gal on a television show who told them if they gave money, they'd get rich. They'll talk about the big hairdo or outrageous makeup of some televangelist and the absurd things they said and did. They'll talk about someone who was religious but broke their hearts or their promise, or lied and got caught or went to jail, or who cried a lot on camera but it looked like they were faking it. Or they'll talk about someone who told them that God hated who they were or how they acted or who they married or couldn't forgive what they'd done. It's a sad situation, honestly. The only way they can keep from being head-faked anymore is for somebody to give them a taste of the real thing."[15]

It's time to give the people around you a taste of the real thing. That is something we can each do to positively influence the "Seven Mountains" of culture.

The Bereans loved their time in the Word of God. I want to encourage you to be diligent with your time in the Bible. God has so much more for you than you can get from just going to church once or twice a week and hearing someone else talk about the Bible. When you spend time in His Word yourself, your life will change in amazing ways. You'll find joy. You'll discover hope. New opportunities will surface. Redemption will come.

> God has so much more for you than you can get from just going to church once or twice a week and hearing someone else talk about the Bible.

Start scheduling time to be in the Bible. Sometimes, it helps me to literally put it on my calendar. If you are a morning person, make an appointment with God in the mornings. If that doesn't work for you, find a time that does. And don't put pressure on yourself that you have to start with hours a day every day. Start with short blocks of time.

READ THE WORD OF GOD IN COMMUNITY

I've learned that I am much more apt to stick with commitments if I have someone who is sweating, dieting, or studying along with me. Several months ago, Beth and I made a decision to eat healthier. We have cut back on the salty snacks, sweets, and processed foods. Has it been easy? No. But it's been a ton easier doing it together. We have built-in accountability and the challenge is easier.

The Bereans studied the Word of God together. The fact that they met in the synagogue to study the Scriptures tells us that this would have been a very communal, interactive time of learning.

Paul told Timothy, his young protégé, "Devote yourself to the public reading of Scripture."[16] He wanted Timothy to read the Scriptures aloud to others so everyone would hear God's Word together as a community, not just individually.

Historically, Bible study had always been done in community because before the 1500's, very few people had their own copy of the Bible. They didn't have printing presses. They didn't have smartphones and tablets. This would force people to meet in homes and read the Bible together. They would then discuss what they had just read.

Today, we have more Bibles than we know what to do with. This is a good thing, but it can lead to spiritual isolation. So many people view Christianity as a solitary, individual thing. We have our podcast pastors that we listen to during commutes, and personalized Bible study plans on our Bible app.

We view our faith as a very personal part of our lives. In one sense it is, but as I have attempted to show you in this book; it is very much a team sport. Jesus tells us that something special happens when two or three gather in His name. When that happens, He is in the midst of them.[17]

You were not created to do life alone. The Bereans showed us that even studying the Bible is best done together. Don't be a lone ranger in your walk with God. Team up with a friend who will study the Bible with you, even if it's just a few verses or a chapter.

Have you ever been sitting in church or in a Bible study where someone shares something from the same passage you have been studying, but they see something that you didn't see? You immediately think, "I never thought of that!"

By reading and discussing the Word of God in community, we acknowledge our inability to fully grasp what God has said on our own and we learn to appreciate the insights and perspectives of others. It's an amazing thing that we can hear the Spirit's voice through our diverse lenses.

Reading the Bible is similar to eating food. You can eat alone, but you are missing something if you never share it with others. When we study the Bible with others, we are reminded that we are a community. Despite our differences, reading with other believers connects us and helps us remember that we are all united in Jesus Christ.

BE CONSISTENT

The Bereans "received the word with all eagerness, *examining the Scriptures daily* to see if these things were so."[18] (italics mine)

One of the best habits you can develop as a Christian is to spend some time in the Bible every day until it becomes a part of who you are. John Ortberg says that consistent spiritual discipline becomes, "a rhythm for living in which we can grow more intimately connected to God."[19]

When you are in the Bible every day, you will have a greater understanding of who God is and about His purpose for your life. You will have greater influence in the "Seven Mountains" of culture. You will also be better equipped as you face trials and opposition every day.

As I am writing this chapter, I am enjoying a family vacation on the beach in South Carolina. One thing my girls love to do is body board or "boogie board" as we call it. Yesterday they went out to boogie board and catch some waves. Beth and I were just talking on the beach and looked up and the girls weren't there. Within just a few minutes, the current had made them drift probably 50 yards down the coast. It happened in no time!

It's just as easy to drift spiritually. The thing about drifting is that there's nothing you really have to do to drift. By simply doing nothing, the current will move you and you will drift away.

We told our girls to come back to where we were. We told them that if they keep their eyes on us and continually look to where we are, they won't drift as easily. If you don't want to drift spiritually, keep looking to Jesus. Spend time with Him every day.

The Bible says to "Pray without ceasing."[20] That doesn't mean you need to literally be on your knees in prayer around the clock. It's about living with an attitude of prayer. It's about being consistent. Throughout the day, we think about God. We trust Him when things don't make sense. We depend on Him. We thank Him for the good things.

No matter where you are in your walk with God, I hope you will start spending time in His Word. Read it when you are by yourself and when you are with others. Make it a priority in your life because it's not any ordinary book. It is powerful.

The Bible has power to change lives. It delivers people from the grasp of evil. It transforms nations. It revives churches. It brings positive change to cultures and societies.

I'll close this chapter with a great reminder from Rick Warren:

> "The Bible is far more than a doctrinal guidebook. God's Word generates life, creates faith, produces change, frightens the Devil, causes miracles, heals hurts, builds character, transforms circumstances, imparts joy, overcomes adversity, defeats temptation, infuses hope, releases power, cleanses our minds, brings things into being, and guarantees our future forever! We cannot live without the Word of God! Never take it for granted. You should consider it as essential to your life as food."[21]

▶ IN REAL LIFE
TIPS TO HELP YOU SPEND TIME IN THE BIBLE

You want to spend time with God, but it's hard. You're busy. You are spinning 10 plates in the air at once. You only have so many hours in the day. It seems as though spending time with God is the last thing on your to-do list. Here are some tips to help you get into the daily routine:

- Schedule time to read the Bible. What you plan to do, you do.
- Read one Psalm or Proverb every day.
- Use a journal to write down what God is teaching you.
- Don't be afraid to write and highlight in your Bible.
- Purchase a good study Bible.
- Pause and listen. Get in the habit of being quiet and allowing God to speak to you.
- Choose a Bible character and study that one person.
- Purchase a good Bible commentary to get other perspectives and insights on the passages you are reading. My favorite set of commentaries are Thru the Bible with Dr. J. Vernon McGee.
- Get a Bible Dictionary. A Bible Dictionary is actually more like an encyclopedia than a dictionary. It's a great tool in Bible study.
- Remember that more is not always better. Sometimes just read a few verses and meditate on them.
- Listen to the Bible while commuting, exercising, or working around the house.

- Set a goal for yourself. Maybe you want to read one chapter a day or just read for 10 minutes a day.
- Purchase a daily devotional full of short, Bible passages and thoughts that you can read and then think on as you go through your day.
- Choose a plan. For those of you who like some structure, there are a ton of Bible reading plans available online and on places like the Bible app.

CHAPTER 9
DON'T WASTE YOUR LONELINESS

It was the sixth day of creation. God had just finished creating all the animal life. As He had done at each stage of creation, He paused and evaluated His work. "And God saw that it was good."[1] Have you discovered that whenever God does something it is always good? When I was a kid in church, we would sing "God is so good. God is so good. God is so good. He's so good to me."

I find myself saying, "God is good" quite a bit. I catch a flight despite heavy traffic and I say, "God is good!" I get more back on a tax return than I was planning on and I say, "God is good!" The bill from the mechanic isn't as bad as I thought it might be and I say, "God is good!"

The reality is that God really is good! And everything He does is good. When God did something so big as to create something from nothing, it was good! But the truth is that His goodness is all around you, even in the smallest and seemingly insignificant parts of our day.

On that sixth day of creation, God created all the land animals. But, He had one more important task left to do:

> "Then the Lord God formed the man of dust from the ground and breathed into his nostrils the breath of life, and the man became a living creature."[2]

God created man. This part of creation should be very interesting to you because the man that God created was your great, great, great, great, great, great, great, great-grandpa Adam. And he is my grandpa, too. As J. Vernon McGee said, "This means that you and I are cousins, although maybe not kissing cousins."

In Genesis 1:1, God described creation using the Hebrew term *bā'rā*, which means "creating something from nothing." But here, the creation of the first man uses the Hebrew word *yi'ser* which means "formed." God formed man like the work of an artist, a sculptor, or a potter.

Adam was created, or formed, to have fellowship with God and to be the object of His love. But after God placed Adam in the Garden, He saw that there was still something missing. For the first time in the Bible, we hear God describe something as "not good."

> "The LORD God said, 'It is not good that the man should be alone; I will make him a helper fit for him.'"[3]

Adam was alone. God created him with a need to connect with another person. Eve would be the object of Adam's love and would love him in return. With the creation of Eve, Adam's close relationship with God was complemented by a relationship with another person.

Fast forward to today. God never designed people to live in solitude… including you. Just like Adam, you have been made with a need to be loved and to belong. It is all a part of God's perfect design.

> Just like Adam, you have been made with a need to be loved and to belong. It is all a part of God's perfect design.

Pastor Steve DeWitt says:

> "God didn't intend man to be alone. This is why he created Eve and marriage. This is why he instituted the family. This is why the church is called a body. God doesn't want anyone to be alone. Solitary confinement is for prisons, not the church."[4]

ONE IS THE LONELIEST NUMBER

I read a story about a man who wanted to join one of those lonely hearts clubs. He sent them a letter with his photograph and they sent back a note that said, "We are not that lonely."

Harry Nilsson taught us that "One is the Loneliest Number" in this famous song. Even the word "loneliness" itself sounds sad and depressing!

What does it mean to be lonely? I don't know that I need to define it for you, but I will because it will make for something good to underline on this page. Get your pen ready. According to Les Carter, "Loneliness is a feeling of separation, isolation, or distance in human relations. Loneliness implies emotional pain, an empty feeling, and a yearning to feel understood and accepted by someone."[5]

If you are struggling with loneliness, you are not alone. A new report suggests that 36% of all Americans – including 61% of young adults and 51% of mothers with young children – feel "serious loneliness."

Let me pause in the narrative of the book and speak to the pastors and church leaders who are reading. These are two great areas of ministry. If young adults and mothers of young children are some of the loneliest people, how can we address this need and create better opportunities for community in our ministries?

According to the research, one out of three Americans are experiencing loneliness.[6] That means one out of every three people you pass feels isolated and alone. Another study reports that more than half of all people feel that no one really knows them well.[7]

Let me hit pause in the book narrative once again. This creates not only ministry opportunities for the church as a whole, but for each one of us. What can you do to get to know someone better today? How can you be the hands and feet of Jesus? How can you make someone who thinks they are invisible feel noticed and loved?

The thing about loneliness is that it impacts everyone. It is no respecter of persons. You can belong to a church and feel like no one knows who you are. You can be at your family Christmas and feel distanced from your relatives. Young or old, single or married, Christian or non-Christian...loneliness can hit us all.

LONELINESS IN THE BIBLE

Many of the great people of the Bible experienced seasons of loneliness. In a weird sense, this makes me feel good! If some of the heroes of our faith battled loneliness and were overcomers, there is hope for you and me!

> If some of the heroes of our faith battled loneliness and were overcomers, there is hope for you and me!

Leah was the first wife of Jacob. Her sister was his second wife. Leah always felt that her sister was loved more by Jacob – which was true. Can you imagine the loneliness of competing with your sister for your husband's love and attention? Loneliness can often come from the deep wounds of those closest to you.

Hagar was the servant of Sarah. Sarah's jealousy towards her caused Hagar and her son to be cast out into the desert. Hagar sat down to die at one point because she and her son were totally alone and without help. Can you imagine the loneliness she felt from being written off and cast away?

David's path to the throne was challenging and lengthy. Fifteen lonely years passed between the time that he was anointed King and the time that he actually became King. A good amount of this time was spent in the wilderness hiding from King Saul. When he was eventually made King, the loneliness didn't leave. At one point, he said, "I have been forgotten like one who is dead; I have become like a broken vessel."[8] All the wealth and power of a King can't substitute for real connections with people.

Naomi said to Ruth and Orpah, "Turn back, my daughters; go your way, for I am too old to have a husband."[9] Naomi anticipated a life of bitter loneliness since losing her husband and her sons. Some of you have experienced the desperate loneliness of grief.

The prophet Jeremiah experienced the pain of rejection and loneliness. God told him not to marry. He had few friends. On top of that, God called him to speak out against the sinfulness of God's people and warn of coming judgment unless they changed their ways. Jeremiah is known by many as the "weeping prophet." He endured the absence of a family, constant social rejections, and a thankless and despised job. I think it's fair to say that would drive anyone to loneliness!

Even Jesus Himself felt isolated at times. Think about His 12 disciples. He spent three years pouring into them; yet they were often selfish, ambitious, unspiritual, and lacking in faith. When Jesus needed them most the night before He died, He asked them to "watch and pray" with Him. Three times, He had to wake them up when they all fell asleep. You can feel alone even while around a small group of people who are supposed to be your closest friends.

PERSECUTION, PAIN, AND PLENTY OF LONELINESS

Paul had come to the end of a rich, full life. We have talked a lot about him in this book. He was one of the most influential leaders of the early church. He played a crucial role in spreading the Gospel during the first century. His missionary journeys took him all throughout the Roman empire. He has to be one of the most influential people in history.

> "Paul's life was remarkable and there is little doubt that it changed the course of Christianity. He made an impact as an apostle, theologian, and letter-writer. Paul the apostle had expanded the church far and wide, flinging open the doors to Gentiles; strenuously fighting for his conviction that the gospel was for all people and that no barriers should be put in the way of Gentiles. Paul the theologian was the first to work through many of the intriguing questions that Jesus' life, death, and resurrection had thrown up. And Paul, the letter-writer, gave us not only some of the profoundest pieces of early Christian theological

reflection; but also some of the finest, most poignant writing in history."[10]

Paul's Christian life had both an incredible beginning and incredible ending. The book of 2 Timothy contains his final words. When you get to the final chapter, there is something in his tone that indicates he knew his life and ministry were coming to an end. These words contain some of the most beautiful (and solemn) words in the Bible.

When writing this chapter, I went back and forth on whether to include the full text of 2 Timothy 4. I have decided to include it. Please don't be tempted to skip over it and move on to what I have to say next. Read Paul's words slowly and it will make the rest of the chapter much more meaningful. Read them as if you were standing behind Paul's shoulders as he wrote them in that cold, dark Roman prison.

"I charge you in the presence of God and of Christ Jesus, who is to judge the living and the dead, and by His appearing and His kingdom: preach the word; be ready in season and out of season; reprove, rebuke, and exhort, with complete patience and teaching. For the time is coming when people will not endure sound teaching, but having itching ears they will accumulate for themselves teachers to suit their own passions, and will turn away from listening to the truth and wander off into myths. As for you, always be sober-minded, endure suffering, do the work of an evangelist, fulfill your ministry.

For I am already being poured out as a drink offering, and the time of my departure has come. I have fought the good fight, I have finished the race, I have kept the faith. Henceforth there is laid up for me the crown of righteousness, which the Lord, the righteous judge, will award to me on that day, and not only to me but also to all who have loved His appearing.

Do your best to come to me soon. For Demas, in love with this present world, has deserted me and gone to Thessalonica. Crescens has gone to Galatia, Titus to Dalmatia. Luke alone is with me. Get Mark and bring him with you, for he is very useful to me for ministry. Tychicus I have sent to Ephesus. When you come, bring the cloak that I left with Carpus at Troas, also the books, and above all the parchments. Alexander the coppersmith did me great harm; the Lord will repay him according to his deeds. Beware of him yourself, for he strongly opposed our message. At my first defense no one came to stand by me, but all deserted me. May it not be charged against them! But the Lord stood by me and strengthened me, so that through me the message might be fully proclaimed and all the Gentiles might hear it. So I was rescued from the lion's mouth. The Lord will rescue me from every evil deed and bring me safely into His heavenly kingdom. To Him be the glory forever and ever. Amen.

Greet Prisca and Aquila, and the household of Onesiphorus. Erastus remained at Corinth, and I left Trophimus, who was ill, at Miletus. Do your best to come before winter. Eubulus sends greetings to you, as do Pudens and Linus and Claudia and all the brothers.

The Lord be with your spirit. Grace be with you."[11]

There is a lot packed in these 22 verses. Paul had a rich and full life, but it came with persecution and pain and plenty of loneliness. Consider the following:

- **His Surroundings:** This last letter from Paul was not written from the comforts of a coffee shop or on the banks of the reservoir. He is in Rome, alone and incarcerated in that horrible Tullianum dungeon.
- **His Company:** Paul was used to being with groups of people that he was either ministering to or currently visiting with. Now he is lonely and the hours are long. He asked Timothy to bring him his books, and especially his parchments.
- **The Time of the Year:** This was just days before winter would set in. He asked Timothy to bring him his winter coat. How are you doing in January? If you're from Indiana like I am, January is the coldest month of the year. I know I'm getting old because the cold weather sure has a negative effect on me.
- **His Future:** From clues inside and outside this letter, it seems Paul is in Rome awaiting his execution. He says, "the time of my departure has come."[12] He has been imprisoned before for His preaching, but this time, he knew things were different.
- **His Thoughts:** He's filled with nostalgic memories including some dear friends and ministry partners.
- **His Trial:** The date is sometime between 64 and 68 AD. Paul has apparently had a first hearing before Caesar, and is now awaiting a second.

- **His Friends:** He thinks back on his first hearing and said, "At my first defense no one came to stand by me, but all deserted me."[13] The implication here is that, though there were many in Rome who could have come and supported Paul in that difficult, difficult time, no one did. The Christian community had let him down. Can you relate? Do you feel alone in your church? Alone in your marriage? Alone at work?

Although you read words of sadness and loneliness coming from Paul, you also hear a tone of victory as Paul gives his final charge to Timothy. Paul was still doing God's work. He chose not to waste his loneliness.

WHAT CAUSES LONELINESS?

Loneliness is a basic human emotion that has existed since Adam in the Garden of Eden. It has affected people all throughout history and touches each of us today. It doesn't have just one single cause and it is complex and unique to each person. Yet, there are a few contributing factors to loneliness that are somewhat universal in nature.

1. LONELINESS COMES FROM CULTURE.

We no longer live in Norman Rockwell's Main Street America. The idea of living in a small town where we know the neighbors, the teachers, the firemen, and everyone walking down the street seems like a thing of the past.

On the contrary, we live in a seemingly impersonal world. We text each other instead of calling. Our friends are on Facebook. Our banks know us more by our account number than our name. The good news is that people give you a number, but God gives you a name. Jesus said, "The sheep hear His voice, and He calls His own sheep by name." (John 10:3) He wants you to know other people by their name, as well.

How many people on your street do you know very well? Stop and think about it.

Remember when they used to build houses with big front porches and small cement pads at the back door? That's because people valued sitting on the front porch and getting to know their neighbors.

Now it's the opposite. We park in an attached garage and make it inside the house without ever having to talk to anyone. Once inside, we screen our calls and get annoyed if someone other than Amazon delivery or UberEats knocks on the front door. We put small cement pads at our front door and construct big decks and outdoor kitchens in the back. We build big privacy fences to keep people out. In the privacy of our backyard, we scroll and swipe on our phones to see what our "friends" are doing.

2. LONELINESS COMES FROM LEADING.

Sometimes one of the greatest sources of loneliness is your job – especially if you are a leader. There's some truth to the saying, "It's lonely at the top."

Peter Drucker, the guru of modern-day management, says that "the four toughest jobs in the United States are to be the President of the U.S.A., to be the President of a major university, to be the chief administrator of a large hospital, and to be the pastor of a church." What makes these jobs so tough? It's not the hours. It's the burden of people constantly coming to them for help and direction.

Leading isn't easy! Leaders often carry the burdens of the people they serve while having nobody to go to for themselves. They get robbed of time with their family. They become a target of criticism, envy, and blame. They work under a microscope. Leaders are not superheroes, but people often expect them to be.

> Leaders often carry the burdens of the people they serve while having nobody to go to for themselves.

I'm not trying to talk you out of leading. Being a leader is a huge privilege. People place their trust and faith in you. You have the opportunity to be a positive role model to people who look up to you. You are instrumental in shaping people's future.

The leadership expert Warren Bennis says:

> "A leader is not simply someone who experiences the personal exhilaration of being in charge. A leader is someone whose actions have the most profound consequences on other people's lives, for better or for worse, sometimes forever and ever."[14]

Leading is great. As I write this, Beth and I have the opportunity to lead several organizations. We have over 50 employees that look to us for leadership and direction. It's both humbling and exciting. But it can also be extremely lonely.

3. LONELINESS COMES FROM SUFFERING.

Suffering can create loneliness. Has a spouse walked out on you and left you for someone else? Are you facing your first Christmas alone? Is a diagnosis keeping you awake at night? Are you going through a time of physical suffering and you feel that no one understands or really cares?

Paul understood the loneliness that comes from suffering.

> "Can you picture the soldiers as they took Paul along the northeastern flank of the prison, down the stairs called the 'steps of groaning,' and into the gloomy interior, where he was handed over to the public executioner? There, Paul would have been stripped of his outer garments, possibly left naked except for his tunic.
>
> Paul was a notable prisoner, the acknowledged and self-confessed leader of the now-detested Christians – the jailer would never dare to be lenient in any way. Paul was led to a trap door in the floor. The door was lifted, ropes were passed under Paul's armpits, then he would have been lowered into the terrible Tullianum dungeon. When his feet touched the floor, the ropes were drawn up, and the trap door was slammed into place so that he was now in the dark. In Paul's day, the name of that dungeon was spoken in whispers. It was the current horror of its day. That dungeon was a black pit – a literal hole in the ground.
>
> The Tullianum dungeon was damp and chilly. His bed was a clump of stale straw and the floor was deep with filth. There was water, but the air was foul.

Food was lowered to prisoners from time to time – just enough food and minimal subsistence to keep body and soul together. There might have been an occasional kidskin of thin, sour wine. History tells us prisoners had actually been eaten by the rats in that dreadful hole."[15]

Suffering can often produce loneliness in a person's life. It's easy to feel alone, isolated, and detached from others in the middle of your grief. It's easy to think that no one understands what you are going through. It's also easy to think that God is even distant in the middle of your pain.

> It's easy to think that no one understands what you are going through.

Apart from Christ, probably no person in the Bible suffered as much as did Job. His suffering came from nowhere. It made no sense. He lost all of his wealth. He lost all of his children. He lost his health. He lost the love of his wife. He lost the compassion of his friends. But he never really lost his faith in God. He chose not to waste his loneliness. His story is recorded for us so that we will have some help in living through times of suffering and pain.

HOW TO HANDLE LONELINESS

Please do not waste your loneliness! You've heard the saying, "No pain, no gain." If everything was easy, you wouldn't be prepared for the amazing things God has in store for you.

We can learn some timeless lessons from Paul when he was in prison and awaiting his execution. He was alone in a moldy, cold Roman prison. Yet, when you read his words, you see him full of faith and confidence in the Lord. He didn't throw a pity party. He didn't complain or give up. Instead, he chose not to waste his loneliness.

1. TAKE CARE OF YOURSELF.

Paul instructed young Timothy:

> "When you come, *bring the cloak that I left with Carpus at Troas*, also the books, and above all the parchments."[16] (italics mine)

This tells us that it is likely that Paul was arrested at Troas, resulting in this second and final imprisonment at Rome. In those days the arresting soldiers had claim to any extra garments in the possession of the person arrested. It may be that Paul was given a heads-up about the arrest and chose to leave a few books and his cloak to the care of a friend named Carpus.

A cloak was a circular cape which fell down below the knees that had an opening for the head. This would definitely be something you would want sitting in a cold prison. Since it was cold in Rome and was getting even colder, he later added, "Do your best to come before winter."[17]

Keeping yourself warm in a cold place is a basic essential when it comes to taking care of yourself. It's important to stay warm so you are comfortable and you don't get sick, right? Even though caring for yourself should come naturally for all of us, it's easy to not take care of yourself when you're down.

Paul teaches you to take care of yourself when you are lonely. I'm talking about the way you eat, sleep, spend your time, and so on. The next time you are facing loneliness, here are some essentials that you don't want to forget.

- **Sleep well.** Getting too little or too much sleep can have a big impact on how you feel. Most adults need a good 8 hours of sleep a night. If you are having problems sleeping, limit the sugar and caffeine before bed, turn off the notifications on your phone, and make sure your bedroom is quiet and dark.
- **Eat right.** A daily diet of sugar, preservatives, and highly processed food can have negative impacts on your physical and emotional health.[18] Do your best to eat clean.
- **Stay hydrated.** According to the Mayo Clinic, men need to drink about 15.5 cups of fluids a day.[19] Women need about 11.5 cups a day. It's crazy how much better I feel when I drink water like I should.
- **Exercise.** Exercise can be really helpful for your spiritual, physical, and mental health. Try to get in at least 30 minutes of moderate physical activity every day.
- **Get outside.** Don't lock yourself inside. Take a walk. Ride your bike. Take a picnic to the park. Getting outside has a great way of clearing your head.
- **Volunteer.** Dedicate a day to working with the elderly, tutoring some kids, or volunteering at the church. These things will help keep you away from the self-centered mindset that loneliness can bring on.

- **Pick up the phone.** Call someone you love and who cares about you. Let them know that you are thinking about them and check in.

At some point in your life, you are going to experience pain. Don't just go through it, grow through it. It starts by taking care of yourself.

> At some point in your life, you are going to experience pain. Don't just go through it, grow through it.

2. SERVE OTHERS.

Sitting in prison and facing execution by Nero, Paul wrote:

> "When you come, bring the cloak that I left with Carpus at Troas, *also the books*, and above all the parchments."[20] (italics mine)

Paul asked Timothy to bring him his books. He decided to take advantage of his down time to study and write. He wrote most of the New Testament during his times in prison. Many of these prison letters ironically (or better yet, supernaturally) deal with some of the most liberating truths ever spoken. Maybe the only way God could slow Paul down so he would write was to put him in prison or solitary confinement.

The Bible says "It is not good for the man to be alone."[21] Even though it's not good to be alone, I promise you will experience loneliness at some point. When you do, you have some choices to make. Will you get off your phone? Will you get out of that pity party? Will you get out the door to serve others?

Our family loves doing puzzles together. Each spring, Beth finds a few really good 1,000-piece puzzles for us to tackle during summer break. On the front of those boxes, there's a picture of what the puzzle is supposed to look like. Maybe it's a toy store or a beach scene with dolphins jumping in the water. The picture on the box shows you that it's going to be beautiful when it's done.

If you were to take just one piece out of the box by itself, you probably wouldn't call that single piece beautiful. You might call it odd-shaped and boring. However, that one piece has a perfect place in the big picture. When all the pieces come together, that one piece will make sense. Don't sit idle waiting for all the pieces to come together. God sees the big picture and He is working it for your good. He does not make mistakes.

> God sees the big picture and He is working it for your good. He does not make mistakes.

Paul didn't waste his loneliness. Sitting in that prison, he wrote letters (which we still benefit from today) to churches. Just like Paul, God has an amazing design for your life and He has laid out all the pieces down to the smallest detail. Don't waste your loneliness. Instead, find ways to serve others.

Giving your time and energy to bless others will help you fight loneliness. Studies show that volunteering and serving the needs of people will ease stress and reduce feelings of loneliness. Along the way, you'll also make new friends and be a happier person.

The Bible says that Job's healing began when he started praying for his friends. When he got his eyes off his own problems and started thinking about others a change came in his life.

3. MAKE THE MOST OF YOUR TIME.

Paul went on to say:

> "When you come, bring the cloak that I left with Carpus at Troas, also the books, *and above all the parchments.*"[22] (italics mine)

Paul was a people person. He didn't like to be alone – it wasn't the way God had wired him. Being in solitary confinement in a dark Roman prison was the opposite of where he wanted to be. Yet, he wasn't going to waste his time.

Paul stayed a student to the end. He wanted Timothy to bring him his books. He especially wanted the parchments, which were portions of the Old Testament. He didn't waste his loneliness.

Paul told the Ephesians to, "make the best use of the time, because the days are evil."[23] Make every minute count. The best way not to waste time is to spend it doing what God wants you to do.

The year was 1536. William Tyndale was once arrested and put in prison just outside of Brussels. He was arrested for putting the Bible into English. His crime was helping people read the Bible in their own language. Just a year before he was strangled and burned at the stake, he sat in prison and wrote these words:

> "I beg your lordship that if I am to remain here through the winter, you will request the commissary to have the kindness to send me from the goods of mine, which he has, a warmer coat also. For this which I have is very thin. A piece of cloth too, to patch my leggings. But most of all, I beg and beseech

your clemency to be urgent with the commissary that he will kindly permit me to have the Hebrew Bible, the Hebrew grammar, and a Hebrew dictionary, that I may pass the time in that study."

William Tyndale chose not to waste his loneliness. Like Paul, he stayed a student until the very end. He didn't want to waste a single minute.

Think about how much time gets wasted every day. One of the biggest reality checks for me is the weekly Screen Time notifications I receive on my phone. I am always amazed that I spend that much time on my phone. Maybe you're in the same boat. Or maybe for you it's watching sports or something else on TV. If you're not careful, too much screen time will cause your brain and your body to vegetate. Use that same time to play in the backyard with your kids, to study the Bible, or to pray for people.

4. DON'T WITHDRAW FROM PEOPLE.

When loneliness creeps up in your life, it may be tempting to withdraw from others. Your natural reaction might be to pull back and wait for someone to reach out to you. This online world we live in makes it so easy to withdraw. All you need is your phone and some Airpods to create a virtual reality that is distanced from everyone around you.

Instead of waiting for someone to reach out to you, I want you to turn that around. Ask the Holy Spirit to give you supernatural strength and wisdom about who you can reach out to yourself.

Community is God's answer to loneliness.

I read a story about a man who was stranded on a desert island for many years. One day while strolling along the beach, he spotted a ship in the distance. This had never happened in all the time he was on the island and he was very excited about the chance of being rescued.

He built a fire on the beach and generated as much smoke as possible. It worked! The ship started heading his way. When it was close enough to the island, a small boat was dispatched to investigate the situation. The man on the island was overjoyed with the chance to meet his rescuers. After some preliminary chit chat, they asked him how he had survived for so many years.

He replied by telling of his exploits for food and how he was able to make a home to live in. In fact, he said, "You can see my home from here. It's up there on the ridge."

He pointed the men in the direction of his home. They looked up and saw three buildings. They asked about the building next to his house and he replied, "That's my church. I go there to worship on Sundays."

When asked about the third building, he replied, "That's where I used to go to church."

Your loneliness may have come from past hurts from people who were supposed to be on your team. Those unresolved hurts and bitterness can lead to loneliness.

We've all had bad things happen to us. A friend did you wrong. The company let you go. A coworker took the credit for your idea. It's easy to go through life offended and hurt. Because we hold on to these unresolved hurts, they turn into grudges.

A grudge is an unwillingness to forgive. Someone has hurt you in the past and you carry it with you every single day.

Here's the thing about grudges. The longer you carry them the heavier they get. You think you are hurting the person that hurt you, but in reality the only person getting hurt is you.

The best thing to do is choose to forgive, drop it, and refuse to pick it back up.

5. PRACTICE HIS PRESENCE.

Thinking about the goodness of God even in his loneliness, Paul wrote:

> "At my first defense no one came to stand by me, but all deserted me. May it not be charged against them! But the Lord stood by me and strengthened me, so that through me the message might be fully proclaimed and all the Gentiles might hear it. So I was rescued from the lion's mouth. The Lord will rescue me from every evil deed and bring me safely into His heavenly kingdom. To Him be the glory forever and ever. Amen."[24]

Though there were many in Rome who could have come and supported Paul during that difficult time, no one did. Paul said that they deserted him. This word "deserted" is the same Greek word Jesus used on the cross when He cried, "My God! My God! Why have you forsaken me?" It's a very strong word. Everyone who could have and should have stood with Paul forsook him.

I'm sure they were full of fear and were scared to associate with someone on trial before Caesar himself. Fear can get the best of all of us. It's easy for any one of us to choose self-preservation over doing the courageous thing for someone else. We have all been on the giving and the receiving side of this.

While it may have appeared that Paul was all alone, we know that he wasn't. Even when no one stood by him in his trial, there was One who always stood by him – the Lord.

One of the most wonderful promises in the Bible is this:

> "He has said, 'I will never leave you nor forsake you.' So we can confidently say, 'The Lord is my helper; I will not fear; what can man do to me?'"[25]

Elisabeth Elliott, who lost her husband (Jim) early in their marriage to the Auca Indians in South America, said out of her experience: "When you are lonely too much stillness is exactly the thing that seems to be laying waste your soul, but use that stillness to quiet your heart before God. Get to know Him." She was saying, "Don't waste your loneliness!"

Paul told the church at Ephesus:

> "For this reason I bow my knees before the Father, from whom every family in heaven and on earth is named, that according to the riches of His glory *He may grant you to be strengthened with power through His Spirit in your inner being, so that Christ may dwell in your hearts through faith.*"[26] (italics mine)

Never forget that you have a friend in Jesus. His presence will more than supply everyone's absence. Don't waste your loneliness!

▶ Never forget that you have a friend in Jesus. His presence will more than supply everyone's absence.

GOD IS IN YOUR CORNER

Do you feel all alone? Do you see no end in sight? Change your perspective! That loneliness is not permanent. It is not there to stop you, it is there to advance you.

On your own, you may feel hopeless. The good news is that you are not on your own! The prophet Isaiah once delivered these words from God:

> *"Fear not, for I am with you*; be not dismayed, for I am your God; I will strengthen you, I will help you, I will uphold you with my righteous right hand."[27] (italics mine)

"Fear not, for I am with you" is both a command and a promise. You don't have to be afraid because God has told you, "I am with you." What more do you need? As Paul said, "If God is for us, who can be against us?"[28]

Last Christmas we got together at my parent's house. We ate and then started the gift exchange. My mom gave me a card that I read out loud. Inside it had these words printed on it, "I couldn't imagine loving a child any more." I thought it was great. My sister, Christin, sitting next to me about choked in disgust. It made for good memory and a great laugh.

Your loneliness does not catch God by surprise. He loves you. Nothing you can do will make God love you any more or any less. You might as well believe that you're His favorite and He couldn't imagine loving a child any more.

God is at work behind the scenes even in your loneliness. He can make a way where there seems to be no way. He is with you and is in your corner. He hasn't brought you this far to leave you now. Your loneliness may appear to be a setback, but He is going to turn it into a comeback.

God is not limited by what you don't have. The world came into existence by the very words of His mouth. Nothing is too difficult for Him. Let God use your loneliness to help you grow and to bless those around you. Draw near to Him. He is with you and will see you through!

▶IN REAL LIFE
WHEN LONELINESS STRIKES, OPEN YOUR BIBLE

Feeling alone? If you are feeling lonely, you might not know where to turn. You can always turn to the Lord and His Word! Here are 10 great Bible verses to help you remember that God is by your side!

1. "Come to me, all who labor and are heavy laden, and I will give you rest" (Matthew 11:28).

2. "For my father and my mother have forsaken me, but the LORD will take me in" (Psalm 27:10).

3. "Be strong and courageous. Do not fear or be in dread of them, for it is the LORD your God who goes with you. He will not leave you or forsake you" (Deuteronomy 31:6).

4. "Give all your worries and cares to God, for He cares about you" (1 Peter 5:7).

5. "Where shall I go from your Spirit?
Or where shall I flee from your presence?
If I ascend to heaven, you are there!
If I make my bed in Sheol, you are there!
If I take the wings of the morning
and dwell in the uttermost parts of the sea,
even there your hand shall lead me,
and your right hand shall hold me" (Psalm 139:7-10).

6. "And the Lord will guide you continually
and satisfy your desire in scorched places
and make your bones strong;
and you shall be like a watered garden,
like a spring of water,
whose waters do not fail" (Isaiah 58:11).

7. "And my God will supply every need of yours according to His riches in glory in Christ Jesus" (Philippians 4:19).

8. "Draw near to God, and he will draw near to you" (James 4:8).

9. "When you pass through the waters, I will be with you;
and through the rivers, they shall not overwhelm you;
when you walk through fire you shall not be burned,
and the flame shall not consume you" (Isaiah 43:2).

10. "He heals the brokenhearted and binds up their wounds" (Psalm 147:3).

CHAPTER 10
THE POWER OF MENTORSHIP

It's the smallest of events that change the course of history. In his book *Napoleon's Hemorrhoids and Other Small Events that Changed History* (great name by the way), Phil Mason documents dozens of small happenings over the centuries. Many of these seemed insignificant at the time, but also seemed to change the course of history.

For example, when Adolf Hitler was only six years old, he experienced such vicious nightmares that his doctor recommended his parents send him to a mental health facility. However, they declined the suggestion, worrying that authorities would discover the abuse his father inflicted upon him. Had he received psychological help at this young age, he may have been mentally sound later in life.

Though everyone today knows that President Franklin Roosevelt suffered from polio, the doctor he visited when he first experienced symptoms misdiagnosed him and subjected him to two weeks of deep massaging. This treatment unfortunately made the disease worse, and ultimately cost him the use of his legs. Had he been properly diagnosed, he may have received treatment that could have more positively influenced his health in the long run, and possibly even bought him a few more years to see the end of World War II and the resulting negotiations.

One of the crew masters aboard the Titanic was replaced at the last minute before the ship began its voyage. Unfortunately, he forgot to hand over the key to the locker which held the binoculars to the new crew master. Had the crew had access to binoculars, it is possible they would have seen the iceberg in time to steer clear of it.

It is indeed the smallest of events that change the course of history. Another seemingly small event happened much earlier on a Mediterranean island called Cyprus. On this island lived a Jewish man named Joses who came to trust Jesus as his Lord and Savior. We don't know how he came to faith in Jesus. Perhaps he was among the visitors to Jerusalem during the Passover and was one of the 3,000 who heard Peter's first sermon. We aren't sure of the details, but Jesus changed his life… and as a result the course of history.

Joses began learning more about Jesus and actively living out his faith. One day, he sold a field he owned and gave the money to meet the needs of the church. Following the custom of the day, the church leaders gave Joses a new name, Barnabas, which meant Son of Encouragement.

It was Barnabas who came to Saul after his Damascus Road experience and mentored him in his faith. If it weren't for Barnabas, who knows what would have happened to Saul or the early church. He defended Paul, traveled with him, and eventually empowered him to lead in the church. Paul did amazing things, but don't forget the one who mentored him. Without Barnabas, there would be no Paul.

In this final chapter of the book, I want to remind you about the importance of having a mentor relationship with someone. In about every field, whether it's church, business, sports, or health; researchers and practitioners alike agree that mentors matter. Oprah Winfrey had it right when she said, "For every one of us that succeeds, it's because there's somebody there to show you the way out."

No matter how smart, talented, or experienced you may be; you will never achieve your God-given destiny without some guidance along the way.

> You will never achieve your God-given destiny without some guidance along the way.

You've likely experienced the power of a mentor at some point in your life. It may have been a high school coach pushing you to train harder, a college professor who guided you down a career path, a pastor who helped you during a tough season of marriage, or a new boss at work helping you succeed in your new job.

I know Beth has fond memories of her Grandpa Rickner. He was more than a pastor and a grandfather to her. He was a mentor in so many areas of her life. He was someone she could talk to about anything from the Bible to politics to plumbing and everything in between. He would actually slow down, listen, and engage in a meaningful conversation – just like a good mentor.

Mentors really do matter.

20 YEARS STRONG

We have spent a lot of time in these pages talking about the Apostle Paul. Once Paul left his mentor, Barnabas, he found someone to mentor himself in a teenager named Timothy. Paul met Timothy while he was traveling through Lystra. His father was a Greek man and we know nothing of his faith. But Timothy's mom and grandmother were faithful Jewish women who, day in and day out, taught him the Old Testament.[1] As the women heard Paul preach, they trusted Jesus as their Lord and Savior, and Timothy did the same.

Timothy may have seen Paul heal a lame man in his town. Can you imagine being an eyewitness to such a miracle? You would never forget it! He may also have watched as that angry mob threw stones at Paul and left him for dead.[2] He may have witnessed God miraculously revive him afterwards. When he came back to Lystra a couple of years later on his second missionary journey, he invited Timothy to travel with him.

The two spent a lot of time together. Timothy traveled with both Paul and Silas on their missionary journeys to the Thessalonians and the Corinthians. Their relationship deepened to the point that Paul called Timothy "my true son in the faith."[3] Paul's confidence in him continued to grow to the point that Paul said, "…I have no one like him, who will be genuinely concerned for your welfare… as a son with a father he has served with me in the gospel…"[4]

Paul and Timothy had a mentoring relationship that extended for 20 years. Friendships like that are special. Sometimes we don't have the same set of friends throughout our entire lives. We relocate, we change jobs, we drift apart, and sometimes we outgrow each other. This is perfectly normal. But there's something special about the friends you've had for decades. They just get you. They've seen you at your best. They've seen you at your worst. Yet there they are.

Paul and Timothy had this kind of relationship. Together, they established churches at Philippi, Thessalonica, and Berea.[5] When Paul left Berea to go to Athens, he left Timothy and Silas behind. Later he sent word for them to join him.[6] Timothy was sent to Thessalonica to strengthen the church community there.[7] Timothy learned how to minister to the church by watching Paul do it. Paul thought of Timothy, not only as a very faithful friend, but as his mentee and spiritual son.

Their relationship serves as a blueprint for us to follow as we build meaningful relationships in this virtual world.

BE AN EAGLE, NOT A CHICKEN

John Maxwell says, "A self-made leader doesn't make much."[8] I don't know of truer words ever spoken. If you have experienced any success in your personal or professional life, it is because there have been people investing in you. And who are they? Mentors.

A mentor is a person who gives you the tools, guidance, support, and feedback you need to grow and improve. According to the Oxford English Dictionary, a mentor is "an experienced person who advises and helps somebody with less experience over a period of time."[9] Some mentoring relationships are for an hour, some are for a season, and some are for a lifetime.

▶ A mentor is a person who gives you the tools, guidance, support, and feedback you need to grow and improve.

I would not be the person I am today without mentors in my life. I learned how to teach adults from a college professor, Keith Drury. I learned sales from watching my dad. I learned marketing from my wife, Beth. I learned how to pastor from my father-in-law, Terry Bishir. I learned corporate board governance from Jack Eggar. I learned real estate investing from Caleb Crandall. I learned how to operate car washes from Bill Corey. These people are mentors in my life.

The concept of mentoring is at least as old as the book of Deuteronomy in the Old Testament.

Moses said:

> "Hear, O Israel: The LORD our God, the LORD is one. You shall love the LORD your God with all your heart and with all your soul and with all your might. And these words that I command you today shall be on your heart. *You shall teach them diligently to your children, and shall talk of them when you sit in your house, and when you walk by the way, and when you lie down, and when you rise.* You shall bind them as a sign on your hand, and they shall be as frontlets between your eyes. You shall write them on the doorposts of your house and on your gates."[10] (italics mine)

In these verses, God laid out mentoring within the family to ensure that faith in the true and living God would be passed from generation to generation.

Fast forward to the New Testament. Jesus chose twelve men to "be with Him."[11] He mentored those early disciples by spending time with them. They ate together, traveled together, and ministered together. They were best friends. Jesus poured His life into these men so they would pour their lives into others.

As we will discuss in this chapter, Barnabas found someone to mentor in Paul, and in return Paul found someone to mentor in young Timothy. When you have a mentor, and in return you mentor someone else, the results are life-changing.

> When you have a mentor, and in return you mentor someone else, the results are life-changing.

Pastor Daniel Stegeman says:

> "Everyone needs a Paul, a Barnabas, and a Timothy in life. This saying carries a pretty simple meaning, but when applied, it can be transformative. One way of explaining this would be to say, everyone needs a mentor, an associate, and an apprentice. We all need someone to build into our lives and mentor us, we all need someone who can labor and work alongside us, and we need someone to whom we can pass on the wisdom and knowledge God has given us. And we probably need more than just one person in each of these categories in our lives."[12]

Paul told the Corinthians, "Be imitators of me, as I am of Christ."[13] The NIV says it this way, "Follow my example, as I follow the example of Christ." He knew the Corinthian Christians needed examples, and he was willing to be such an example.

Paul would later tell Timothy to do the same thing:

> "Let no one despise you for your youth, *but set the believers an example* in speech, in conduct, in love, in faith, in purity."[14] (italics mine)

Sometimes the best thing you can do with your time and with your life is to just be a good example for people. This is the heart of mentoring.

Every person – including you – needs mentors and models. You need someone whose hindsight can become your foresight... someone who is just ahead of where you are in your growth and life journey. Whether it's in your business, your ministry, your finances, your job, your marriage, or your personal walk with the Lord; a mentor can make all the difference.

> You need someone whose hindsight can become your foresight... someone who is just ahead of where you are in your growth and life journey.

Mentors lift you and inspire you. My girls love roller coasters. At Dollywood, their favorite coaster is Wild Eagle. It stands 21 stories above Dollywood and makes you feel like you are actually soaring high above the Smoky Mountains. If you're a coaster enthusiast, it's a great ride. Our Londyn loves it so much that she bought a t-shirt in the gift shop where you exit the ride that says, "Be an eagle, not a chicken." She wears it to school.

Here's the thing. You're going to become like whomever you're connected to. Are you connected to eagles or chickens?

Joel Osteen says:

> "You can't hang out with chickens and expect to soar with eagles. You're going to become like the people you associate with."[15]

You need to invite eagles into your life that can help you soar. Then in return you need to be an eagle for someone coming behind you.

Jim Rohn put it well:

> "Don't take the casual approach to life. Casualness leads to casualties. Seek out the mentors that you need that will lead you to greatness in your field. If you're not willing to learn from others, who are you willing to learn from?"[16]

This is what being friends in real life is all about. As Andy Stanley says, "The value of a life is always measured by how much of it is given away." Making small investments of time in the lives of others will always reap big dividends.

MENTORING WORKS

John Crawford Crosby said, "Mentoring is a brain to pick, an ear to listen, and a push in the right direction."[17] Finding someone that will support and encourage you can change the trajectory of your life.

Dr. Howard Hendricks used to say that every Christian needs at least three people in their life. You need someone who has come before you who can mentor you. You need another beside you to share your burden. And you need someone behind you whom you are mentoring. Otherwise, you'll grow stagnant.

The benefits of having a mentor are widely documented. Research shows that:

- 97% of people with a workplace mentor say it's valuable.
- 89% of those who have been mentored will also go on to mentor others.

- 25% of employees who enrolled in a mentoring program had a salary grade change, compared to only 5% of workers who did not participate.
- Mentees were 5 times more likely to be promoted.
- 67% of businesses reported an increase in productivity due to mentoring.[18]

Mentoring not only works, but it has supernatural results. One of my favorite Bible characters is Noah. The Bible says that he "found favor in the eyes of the LORD."[19] God described Noah as a righteous man, meaning he treated people right and he tried to please the Lord with his life. As I'm sure you know, God told him to build that big floating zoo. When the great flood came and covered the earth, Noah and his family were the only ones saved.

What's interesting is that the Bible never says that his children found favor in God's eyes. It only says that of Noah. But because they were connected to Noah, their lives were spared.

There's a principle here that I don't want you to miss. When you are connected to someone with God's favor, that favor is going to flow down on you. Joel Osteen preaches a great message on this titled "Favor Connections." It's worth looking up and listening to. When you connect to people who are more successful than you, success will flow down on you. When you connect with people who are smarter than you, those smarts will flow down on you. When you connect with people who are being blessed, those blessings will flow down on you.

I'll never forget the week that my pastor asked me to teach children's church for the first time. I was 18 years old and still in high school. I was a nervous wreck! I couldn't sleep the night before. Thankfully, I had a youth pastor who had experience teaching kids. He mentored me. He coached me on what to do and what not to do. He gave me the confidence that I could do it.

MAKE A LIFE BY WHAT YOU GIVE

Winston Churchill famously said, "We make a living by what we get, but we make a life by what we give."[20]

God blesses generous people who give. Proverbs says, "Those who give generously receive more."[21] Paul shared a similar truth when he said, "Whoever sows sparingly will also reap sparingly, and whoever sows bountifully will also reap bountifully… God loves a cheerful giver."[22]

When we give, we are to give generously because the way we give is the way we receive. This applies to more than just our money. It also includes our time – which is your most valuable asset.

The Bible is filled with stories of people who gave their time to others. They have the tools, guidance, support, and feedback needed to grow and improve.

Jethro mentored Moses and in return Moses mentored Joshua. Eli mentored Samuel and then Samuel went on to mentor David. Barnabas mentored Paul then Paul mentored Timothy. This is how God has designed the chain of mentorship to work.

Paul told Timothy, "What you have heard from me in the presence of many witnesses entrust to faithful men, who will be able to teach others also."[23] Paul challenged Timothy to take the things he had learned and teach them to others who could then teach others also. See the chain of mentorship?

So where do you start?

STEP 1: CHOOSE TO MAKE TIME.

It begins with a decision to take the experiences of my life and generously help another person. John Maxwell says, "A mentor is someone with a head full of experience and heart full of generosity that brings those things together for another person."

Choosing to make time to help someone else might sound like something for an expert or someone with years of success under their belt. But that's not the case. If you have a relationship with Christ, a love for people, and life experiences (both good and bad); that's all it takes.

What is our nation's greatest natural resource? Is it the wood in our forests? The mineral oil under the sea? Walt Disney said it's the minds of our children. These are each valuable, but they pale in comparison to the worth of your influence in someone's life. You just have to decide to make time to do it.

The biggest challenge you will face after deciding to mentor someone is time. Your schedule will fill up and you won't seem to have the time to invest in someone else. This is why you have to choose to make the time.

Paul felt this tension. In addition to being an evangelist, church planter, and writer of most of the New Testament; he chose to be bi–vocational. Actually, I would call him multi-vocational! He supported himself financially by being a tent-maker on top of everything else he had going on. Even though he was busy with ministry and making tents, he made time to mentor those around him.

Our lives can get way too busy. I hear it all the time as I am sure you do. I'll ask someone, "How are you?" Nine times out of ten, what's the response? "Busy!"

We aren't just busy – we're too busy. But why? I recently read an article that shared 7 hypotheses for why we are so busy.

I thought they were very thought-provoking and so I want to share them with you:

- **Busyness as a badge of honor and trendy status symbol** — or the glorification of busy — to show our importance, value, or self-worth in our fast-paced society.
- **Busyness as job security** — an outward sign of productivity and company loyalty.
- **Busyness as FOMO (Fear of Missing Out)** — spending is shifting from buying things ("have it all") to experiences ("do it all"), packing our calendars (and social media feeds with the "highlight reel of life").
- **Busyness as a byproduct of the digital age** — our 24/7 connected culture is blurring the line between life and work; promoting multitasking and never turning "off".
- **Busyness as a time filler** — in the age of abundance of choice, we have infinite ways to fill time (online and off) instead of leaving idle moments as restorative white space.
- **Busyness as necessity** — working multiple jobs to make ends meet while also caring for children at home.
- **Busyness as escapism** — from idleness and slowing down to face the tough questions in life (e.g. Maybe past emotional pain or deep questions like, "What is the meaning of life?" or "What is my purpose?").

Do you see yourself in any of these scenarios? Whatever the reason you find yourself busy, remember the words of

Socrates when he said, "Beware the barrenness of a busy life." Replace that barrenness with a decision to invest in others.

STEP 2: ALLOW OTHERS TO GROW FROM YOUR EXPERIENCES.

Paul told Timothy, "You have followed my teaching, my conduct, my aim in life, my faith, my patience, my love, my steadfastness, my persecutions and sufferings…"[24] Timothy was right beside Paul as he worked in ministry. Paul shared with Timothy what God had given to him.

One of the greatest scientists of his time, Sir Isaac Newton, once said, "If I have seen further it is by standing on the shoulders of giants." Back in 1676, he spoke of the great thinkers who came before him as "giants." Their insights helped him discover new insights of his own.

Three hundred and forty-six years later, the giants are much taller. They're all over the place — not just in books, like in Newton's time. They tweet. They are online. They have podcasts. They might be on the other side of the world, but they are only one LinkedIn message away.

In this virtual world we live in, you can stand on the shoulders of as many giants as you would like. You'll always stand taller and see further ahead than others when you get help from others.

Timothy had the opportunity to stand on the shoulders of Paul as Paul invested time and energy into him. No one gets to the top alone. We all have help.

You might feel like you can't give someone else everything that they need. You're no Apostle Paul or a seasoned veteran with a storehouse of knowledge to share. I have felt this way many times before. One of the greatest lessons I learned about being a mentor came from Andy Stanley when he taught that your goal is not to fill someone else's cup, it is to empty your own cup.

You have a cup. It is filled with a mixture of your personality, education, career, relationship with God, biblical knowledge, prayer life, life experiences, life wisdom, and so on. God has placed people in your life, and your job is just to pour the contents of your cup into theirs.

If the goal of mentoring is emptying your cup, then you have no excuse not to help someone else.

- I don't know enough. FALSE
- I have not been a Christian long enough. FALSE
- I don't have the right personality. FALSE
- I am too young. FALSE
- I am inexperienced. FALSE
- It is not my gifting. FALSE
- I don't have anything to offer. FALSE
- I am not qualified. FALSE

If the goal is to empty your cup, this frees you from the self-imposed pressure to be a know-it-all and give someone every single thing that you think they may need. The power of mentoring is simply sharing what you have, asking the Holy Spirit to do His work, and allowing someone else to grow from your experiences.

▶ The power of mentoring is simply sharing what you have, asking the Holy Spirit to do His work, and allowing someone else to grow from your experiences.

Your job is simply to take what you have and pour it into someone around you. What can you do to help fill someone's cup today?

STEP 3: KEEP THE CHAIN OF MENTORSHIP GOING.

Always take the posture of a mentor and mentee. Life is a journey, not a destination. You never arrive. You need help along the way. Keep the chain of mentorship going by being a mentee and a mentor at the same time.

In a letter to the Romans, Paul said, "Timothy, my fellow worker, greets you."[25] Timothy had gone from being a son to a student and now to being a fellow worker. He was now one of Paul's closest and most trusted associates. Barnabas mentored Paul. Paul mentored Timothy. Timothy in return would mentor others.

Earlier, Paul made a stunning claim to the Romans, "from Jerusalem and all the way around to Illyricum I have fulfilled the ministry of the Gospel of Christ."[26] What makes this so remarkable is that Illyricum was the end of the known world at the time. How did Paul do this without jet planes, live streams, or social media? He did it by mentoring and duplicating himself in others.

As we end this chapter, I would like for you to take an inventory of your life. Who's your Paul? Who is that person actively encouraging you and challenging you in your life? Who's your Timothy? Who are you intentionally investing time into? Are you keeping the chain of mentorship going?

Proverbs says, "As iron sharpens iron, so one person sharpens another."[27] God uses the mentoring relationship to strengthen the lives of each person involved.

If you wish you had a Paul in your life, start looking and asking God to show you someone who can speak into your life. Don't overthink it. Who can you think of who is growing or successful in an area where you're trying to grow? Start there and see how you can access that person's insights. You won't know until you start looking and asking.

You might not even want to ask that person to "mentor" you – at least at the beginning. Start by simply asking them for a few minutes of their time.

Craig Groeschel says:

> "Instead of asking someone to mentor you, consider asking them to lunch or breakfast, or set up a 20-minute chat over coffee. Prepare questions, and then be ready to listen!"[28]

Look for people who can speak into your life and future. Carolyn Everson, the Director of The Coca-Cola Company, recommends you take on a "board of advisors" to help with multiple aspects of your life. No one person will have all the answers, so she recommends choosing a number of different mentors with different backgrounds and experiences to shape your future.[29]

We all know the story of Moses. He was one of the most prominent figures of the Old Testament. He was chosen to bring redemption to His people. But how did it start? It's interesting that although it was Moses' mother that birthed him, it was his mentor that positioned him. He grew up under the influence (and the same roof) as the Pharaoh of Egypt. Sometimes it takes an outsider, or a mentor, to equip you for the work God has placed in front of you.

> ▶ Sometimes it takes an outsider, or a mentor, to equip you for the work God has placed in front of you.

Start praying and asking the Lord to send the right people into your life. But please don't stop with prayer. Be intentional about it. If God lays a person on your heart, then ask them for a few minutes of their time.

Beth and I live in the world of insurance day after day. We help people insure everything from their car to their house to their life. Think of a mentor as people insurance. A mentor is someone you can reach out to in a moment of need. You can ask them for advice. You can ask them for prayer. You'll find the courage and confidence to do things maybe you wouldn't do on your own.

▶ IN REAL LIFE
HAVE A GREAT MENTOR?
HERE'S HOW TO BE A GOOD MENTEE

You have found a mentor. Great work! Your life is only going to get better because a good mentoring relationship is one of the most crucial you will develop in your life. How can you be a better mentee? Here are some tools to help you get the most out of the relationship:

1. Sit in the driver's seat.
Your mentor shouldn't be the one pushing things along. Set up meeting times. Come up with discussion topics. Follow up. Send your questions ahead of time.

2. Be ready.
Respect your mentor's time by being prepared. Do your homework. Show up with questions to make sure the time together is productive.

3. Be you.
Your mentor has taken time to get to you and invest their time into you. You don't need to posture or pretend to be someone you are not. Be real.

4. Learn to listen.
Before speaking, listen. Absorb everything your mentor has to say and take notes if that would help. Most of the successful people I know are better at listening than talking.

5. Be coachable.
Be open to receiving help and guidance. Be willing to learn new things and appreciate other perspectives.

6. Ask good questions.
You should be hungry to learn, improve, and grow. The success of a mentoring conversation depends on the quality – not quantity – of the questions you ask.

7. Add value.
Look for ways to serve the person helping you. Share an article or podcast that your mentor would appreciate or learn from. Offer to help him or her in practical ways.

8. Take action.
Words are great, but actions lead to outcomes. Don't just sit around waiting for things to fall on your lap. Put in the effort and hard work.

9. Ask for feedback.
Feedback is the breakfast of champions. Your mentor is there to help you. Be mature enough to accept feedback as a gift. Manage your ego and allow feedback to help you grow and change.

10. Show gratitude.
Be sure to express your thanks and provide specific feedback about how your mentor has impacted your life. Whether it's before or after being together, in a text, or in an email; a simple "thank you" can go a long way.

NOW WHAT?
CONCLUSION

Beth and I frequently get asked the question, "How do you guys get so much done? What's your secret?" That's a fair question. After all, Beth owns a design company. Together we lead a global children's ministry... and a car wash... and a real estate company... and an insurance agency. Oh yes, we have three amazing girls! We definitely have a lot of plates spinning at any given time.

Our secret is that we don't do it alone. We understand the power of synergy.

The modern concept of synergy was proposed by chemists. They discovered that every time they separated atoms or molecules from a complex compound, the behavior of the separate parts could never explain the behavior of all of them interconnected. For example, the chemical behaviors of isolated hydrogen (H2) and isolated oxygen (O2) do not offer any kind of information about the chemical behavior of water (H2O). Chemists called this principle synergy, a form of collective transmutation that allowed for endless research and innovation in chemistry.[1]

When we think about synergy as it relates to people, we think about the power of people coming together. I always tell people that synergy is when 1+1=3 or 2+2=12. It's the idea that the collective results of a group always exceed the individual contributions themselves.

Stephen Covey says it this way:

> "Synergy is what happens when one plus one equals ten or a hundred or even a thousand! It's the profound result when two or more respectful human beings determine to go beyond their preconceived ideas to meet a great challenge."

When people come together in synergy they are saying, "I can do good things. You can do good things. Together we can do great things!"

The Old Testament says it like this:[2]

> "How should one chase a thousand, and two put ten thousand to flight?"

Slow down and read those words again. "How should one chase a thousand, and two put ten thousand to flight?" Did you catch that? One can chase a thousand. Two can chase ten thousand. Two is not twice as powerful as one, it is ten times as powerful as one! You'll always get more done in community with others.

Beth and I can only accomplish what we do because of God's favor and an amazing team around us. We have deep value and gratitude for our employees and the hundreds of volunteers that work with us. I want the same for you. Learn to value the people God has placed in your life. You will only reach the fullness of your destiny with the help of others.

I'm a to-do list guy. Every day I write down my priorities and I do my best to tackle them. Did you know that the greatest commandment Jesus gave isn't an item that can be checked off a to-do list?

Jesus said:

> "You shall love the Lord your God with all your heart and with all your soul and with all your mind. This is the great and first commandment. And a second is like it: You shall love your neighbor as yourself."[3]

The two greatest commandments are both about love! God made you for relationships. He wants you to love Him first and foremost and then He wants you to love others.

This is my challenge to you as we wrap up this book. Commit to valuing and loving people. Get to the point in your life where it's not a task on your list but a deep-rooted value in your heart. There are enough downers in the world. Choose to be a lifter. Be a friend of faith, not a friend full of judgment and jealousy. Be a dream builder, not a dream dasher.

Jesus said:

> "A new commandment I give to you, that you love one another: just as I have loved you, you also are to love one another."[4]

It's not always easy to love people, but do it anyway. Why? Because Jesus does. He will help you love those around you. Throughout the day pray, "Lord, help me to be your hands and feet. Lord, send people my way that I can speak life over. Lord, help me to be good to people. Lord, make me an encourager, not a critic."

Remember the words of Bob Goff:

> "Every time I wonder who I should love and for how long I should love them, God continues to whisper to me: Everybody, always."[5]

Do everything in your power to build authentic community in a world that is getting more and more connected while growing more and more lonely. Follow the example of Paul and the early church while practicing the principles taught in this book. Do it for everybody, always. It will help you become everything God has created you to be.

▶ IN REAL LIFE
CONTACT RYAN

Get a regular dose of encouragement and inspiration from Ryan. Send him a text at (765) 441-4598.

Ryan frequently speaks at churches, conferences, and conventions throughout the year. He is a thought-provoking ministry and business practitioner rooted in the notion that if you can dream it, you can do it. It's about having the right mindset. Most of his talks are to pastors and ministry leaders. However, he also enjoys speaking on entrepreneurship, building and engaging an audience, and productivity. If you are interested in finding out more, please visit ryanfrank.com/speak.

You can also connect with Ryan on his podcast, Twitter, Facebook, LinkedIn and Instagram. Find all of the links at ryanfrank.com.

▶ ENDNOTES

FOREWORD
1. Exodus 3:7-8

INTRODUCTION
1. Genesis 2:18
2. Proverbs 13:20 (NRSV)
3. Proverbs 27:17 (LEB)
4. https://pastorrick.com/devotional/english/full-post/god-created-you-to-need-other-people1/

CHAPTER 1
1. Proverbs 17:17
2. https://hivelife.com/family-rental-services/
3. Leviticus 26:12
4. 1 Corinthians 12:27
5. Genesis 2:18
6. Psalm 139:14
7. https://www.biblestudytools.com/bible-study/topical-studies/why-is-it-not-good-for-man-to-be-alone.html
8. John 13:35
9. https://abcnews.go.com/Technology/facebook-friends-fewer-close-friends-cornell-sociologist/story?id=14896994
10. https://newsinhealth.nih.gov/2017/02/do-social-ties-affect-our-health
11. https://www.independent.co.uk/extras/lifestyle/social-media-superficial-friends-fake-book-a8758246.html
12. Acts 9:15
13. Colossians 2:1-7
14. Hebrews 10:24-25
15. https://www.christianity.com/christian-life/spiritual-growth/don-t-go-it-alone-you-were-made-for-community.html
16. Proverbs 27:9
17. Proverbs 13:20
18. Proverbs 27:5–6
19. Proverbs 25:11–12

20. https://www.fastcompany.com/3068959/6-ways-to-become-a-better-listener
21. James 1:19
22. James 4:10
23. Bronnie Ware, The Top Five Regrets of the Dying: A Life Transformed by the Dearly Departing, 2012

CHAPTER 2

1. Matthew 21:22
2. Acts 1:4-5, 8
3. Acts 1:13-14
4. Acts 2:1-4
5. https://www.imb.org/2018/11/28/4-things-church-wildfire/
6. https://www.str.org/w/what-we-need-to-learn-about-prayer-from-the-early-church
7. Acts 12:5
8. Rad Zdero, *The Global House Church Movement*, 2013
9. Matthew 18:20
10. https://www.crossway.org/articles/what-george-mueller-can-teach-us-about-prayer/
11. https://www.christianity.com/church/church-history/church-history-for-kids/george-mueller-orphanages-built-by-prayer-11634869.html
12. Psalm 145:18
13. Ephesians 3:12 NLT
14. 2 Chronicles 16:9 NLT
15. Psalm 34:3
16. Matthew 18:19-20
17. Leviticus 26:8
18. John 17:22-23 MSG
19. Galatians 6:2
20. Luke 11:5-13
21. Ecclesiastes 4:9-10
22. James 5:16
23. R.A. Torrey, *The Power of Prayer and the Prayer of Power*, 1924.
24. Jeremiah 29:11-13
25. Wikiquote: "Zig Ziglar" (Quotes)
26. 1 Thessalonians 5:11

CHAPTER 3
1. Acts 2:42-47
2. Acts 2:41
3. Acts 5:28
4. Gene Getz, *The Measure of a Church*, 2002
5. https://www.christianitytoday.com/history/2008/november/why-and-when-did-christians-start-constructing-special.html
6. John 4:19-24
7. https://www.visionroom.com/rick-warren-shares-8-characteristics-healthy-church/
8. Donald Norbie, *The Early Church*, 43
9. https://www.npr.org/sections/thetwo-way/2018/01/17/578645954/u-k-now-has-a-minister-for-loneliness
10. Acts 2:42
11. Luke 24:27
12. 2 Corinthians 10:5
13. Job 8:21 NIV
14. Acts 2:42
15. Proverbs 27:17
16. Acts 2:42
17. Luke 22:17-19
18. Matthew 26:18 MSG
19. Acts 2:42
20. James 5:16
21. John 14:14
22. Matthew 6:9-13
23. Acts 2:44-45
24. Acts 4:37; 5:1,4
25. Luke 19:9
26. https://www.gottman.com/about/research/couples/
27. https://pastorrick.com/learn-to-love-by-being-generous/
28. 2 Corinthians 8:7
29. Acts 2:46
30. Acts 2:46
31. Acts 10:38
32. John 13:14
33. John 13:34

34. Galatians 6:10
35. 1 Timothy 5
36. https://www.ifgathering.com/iftable-legacy/march-2022-refuse-to-live-alone/

CHAPTER 4

1. Kevin M. Watson, *Pursuing Social Holiness*, Oxford University Press, 2015, page 44.
2. Romans 12:4-5
3. 1 Peter 2:9-10
4. https://www.thegospelcoalition.org/article/faithful-citizen-lone-ranger/
5. Acts 13:1-3
6. Revelation 1:3
7. https://www.christianitytoday.com/history/people/denominationalfounders/john-knox.html
8. Billy Graham, Hope for Each Day: Words of Wisdom and Faith
9. Acts 13:48
10. https://www.compellingtruth.org/Paul-first-missionary-journey.html
11. Ecclesiastes 4:9-12
12. Galatians 6:1–2 NLT
13. Philippians 2:1-8 MSG
14. Hebrews 10:24
15. merriam-webster.com/dictionary/paroxysm
16. https://www.gallup.com/workplace/237059/employee-burnout-part-main-causes.aspx
17. https://www.atlassian.com/blog/teamwork/the-importance-of-teamwork
18. https://www.tinypulse.com/2014-employee-engagement-organizational-culture-report
19. https://www.apa.org/news/press/releases/2006/04/group
20. Proverbs 27:17 MSG
21. Stephen Covey, *The SPEED of Trust: The One Thing That Changes Everything*, 2006

CHAPTER 5

1. Hebrews 13:2

2. Ephesians 2:10
3. Luke 14:13-14
4. https://missiodeijournal.com/issues/md-7/authors/md-7-liggin
5. 1 Corinthians 2:3
6. Romans 16:3-4
7. Job 31:32
8. Hebrews 13:2
9. Leviticus 19:34
10. Isaiah 58:6-7 MSG
11. Luke 22:19-20
12. John 14:1-3
13. John 15:4
14. Luke 10:37
15. Matthew 25:31-45
16. https://d2y1pz2y630308.cloudfront.net/25295/documents/2020/5/How%20to%20Change%20the%20World.pdf
17. Martha Stewart, *Entertaining* (New York: Clarkson N. Potter, 1998).
18. 2 Timothy 2:2
19. Karen Mains, *Open Heart, Open Home.*
20. Galatians 6:10 NLT
21. Galatians 1:10 NIV
22. Romans 12:13
23. Genesis 12:1-3
24. Luke 6:38
25. https://www.joelosteen.com/en-US/inspiration/blogs/2018/06/27/21/56/Blessed%20to%20Be%20a%20Blessing
26. Romans 12:13

CHAPTER 6

1. https://www.history.com/this-day-in-history/thomas-jefferson-and-john-adams-die
2. John 15:12
3. John 13:35
4. https://livingontheedge.org/2012/07/02/why-we-are-called-to-be-encouragers/

5. Dwight Pentecost, *Life's Problems, God's Solutions: Answers to Fifteen of Life's Most Perplexing Problems* (Grand Rapids, MI: Kregel, 1998), 86.
6. Hebrews 10:24-25
7. Hebrews 3:13 NIV
8. Colossians 4:8
9. Galatians 6:17
10. 2 Corinthians 11:25
11. Philippians 4:13
12. https://proverbs31.org/read/devotions/full-post/2018/08/27/love-like-that
13. 1 Corinthians 12:31 NLT
14. 1 Corinthians 13:1-13
15. John 15:12
16. https://www.desiringgod.org/messages/the-power-to-risk-in-the-cause-of-christ
17. Proverbs 18:21
18. 1 Thessalonians 5:11
19. https://www.smartinsights.com/social-media-marketing/social-media-strategy/new-global-social-media-research/
20. Romans 14:19 NASB
21. Rick Warren, *The Purpose Driven Life*, 2002
22. Proverbs 12:25
23. 1 John 4:7
24. Hebrews 4:12
25. Romans 15:4
26. Proverbs 15:30 NLT
27. James 1:19
28. Proverbs 18:13
29. Hebrews 3:13 NIV
30. https://www.azquotes.com/quote/1198074

CHAPTER 7

1. https://sapienlabs.org/mentalog/trauma-and-adversity-in-the-general-population/
2. Romans 8:28
3. https://cityonahillstudio.com/6-things-god-wants-to-tell-you-in-the-middle-of-your-pain/
4. Acts 16:17

5. 2 Corinthians 11:23 NIV
6. Acts 16:25
7. Acts 16:30
8. Acts 16:31
9. Psalm 34:19 NIV
10. 1 Corinthians 16:9
11. https://pastorrick.com/you-heal-from-pain-by-helping-others/
12. John 11:35
13. Galatians 6:2
14. Genesis 39:21
15. Psalm 31:7
16. Isaiah 26:3
17. Cynthia Heald, *Becoming a Woman of Simplicity*, 2017
18. Philippians 4:6-7
19. Acts 16:25
20. Acts 19:26 NIV
21. Psalms 22:3
22. Philippians 4:6
23. Romans 5:3
24. https://joycemeyer.org/dailydevo/2019/11/1130-let-your-mess-become-your-message
25. Psalm 66:12 NLT
26. John 15:2
27. Acts 16:25
28. 2 Corinthians 3:2-3 KJV
29. Ecclesiastes 7:8
30. Genesis 37-50
31. https://davidjeremiah.blog/5-surprising-reasons-god-allows-adversity/
32. Psalm 50:15
33. https://abcnews.go.com/International/story?id=81812&page=1
34. Isaiah 43:19
35. Ecclesiastes 4:10 MSG
36. https://joycemeyer.org/everydayanswers/ea-teachings/The-Healing-Power-of-Gods-Word
37. 2 Corinthians 1:4

CHAPTER 8
1. Hebrews 10:24-25
2. https://en.wikivoyage.org/wiki/Veria
3. Acts 17:10-12
4. Acts 17:5 NIV
5. Acts 17:11-12
6. Acts 17:11
7. Proverbs 12:25 TPT
8. Proverbs 19:22 NASB
9. Acts 17:11
10. James 1:19-20
11. Colossians 4:6
12. Acts 17:11
13. Joni Eareckson Tada, *Diamonds in the Dust*
14. Matthew 22:39
15. Bob Goff, *Love Does: Discover a Secretly Incredible Life in an Ordinary World*
16. 1 Timothy 4:13
17. Matthew 18:20
18. Acts 17:11
19. John Ortberg, *The Life You've Always Wanted*
20. 1 Thessalonians 5:16
21. https://www.facebook.com/pastorrickwarren

CHAPTER 9
1. Genesis 1:25
2. Genesis 2:7
3. Genesis 2:18
4. https://www.biblicalcounselingcoalition.org/2011/08/15/lonely-me-a-pastoral-perspective/
5. Les Carter, *Mind Over Emotions*, 121.
6. https://mcc.gse.harvard.edu/reports/loneliness-in-america
7. https://www.health.harvard.edu/blog/the-power-and-prevalence-of-loneliness-2017011310977
8. Psalm 31:12
9. Ruth 1:12
10. https://www.bbc.co.uk/religion/religions/christianity/history/paul_1.shtml

11. 2 Timothy 4
12. 2 Timothy 4:6
13. 2 Timothy 4:16
14. https://www.linkedin.com/pulse/leadership-entitlement-its-privilege-responsibility-gifford-thomas/
15. https://media.faith-bible.net/scripture/2timothy/what-are-your-essentials-a-coat-and-books
16. 2 Timothy 4:13
17. 2 Timothy 4:21
18. https://www.medicalnewstoday.com/articles/318630
19. https://www.mayoclinic.org/healthy-lifestyle/nutrition-and-healthy-eating/in-depth/water/art-20044256#
20. 2 Timothy 4:13
21. Genesis 2:18 NCV
22. 2 Timothy 4:13
23. Ephesians 5:16
24. 2 Timothy 4:16-18
25. Hebrews 13:5-6
26. Ephesians 3:14-17
27. Isaiah 41:10
28. Romans 8:31

CHAPTER 10

1. Acts 16:1; 2 Timothy 1:5
2. Acts 14:8-20
3. 1 Timothy 1:2
4. Philippians 2:19-24
5. Acts 16:1 – 17:14
6. Acts 17:13-15
7. 1 Thessalonians 3:1-2
8. John Maxwell, *Leadership Gold*, 2008
9. https://www.oxfordlearnersdictionaries.com/us/definition/english/mentor
10. Deuteronomy 6:4-9
11. Mark 3:14
12. https://pastoral-theology.com/2011/12/05/everyone-needs-a-paul-a-barnabas-and-a-timothy/
13. 1 Corinthians 11:1
14. 1 Timothy 4:12

15. https://twitter.com/joelosteen/status/871162142237523969
16. Sreechinth C, *Jim Rohn's Success Tips for an Exceptional Living*, page 50
17. https://www.brainyquote.com/quotes/john_c_crosby_137546
18. https://www.togetherplatform.com/blog/how-to-build-a-successful-mentor-relationship
19. Genesis 6:8
20. https://www.brainyquote.com/quotes/winston_churchill_131192
21. Proverbs 11:24 CEB
22. 2 Corinthians 9:6–7
23. 2 Timothy 2:2
24. 2 Timothy 3:10-11
25. Romans 16:21
26. Romans 15:19-20
27. Proverbs 27:17 NIV
28. https://www.facebook.com/craiggroeschel/posts/1176941939031055/
29. Paul Springer and Mel Carson, *Pioneers of Digital*, 2012

CONCLUSION

1. https://www.forbes.com/sites/luisromero/2015/12/01/the-ultimate-guide-to-team-synergy
2. Deuteronomy 32:30
3. Matthew 22:37-39
4. John 13:34
5. Bob Goff, *Everybody, Always: Becoming Love in a World Full of Setbacks and Difficult People*

www.ingramcontent.com/pod-product-compliance
Lightning Source LLC
Chambersburg PA
CBHW050325010526
44119CB00038B/471/J